The Gentrification of the Internet

The Gentrification of the Internet

HOW TO RECLAIM OUR DIGITAL FREEDOM

Jessa Lingel

UNIVERSITY OF CALIFORNIA PRESS

University of California Press
Oakland, California

Library of Congress Cataloging-in-Publication Data

Names: Lingel, Jessa (Jessica), author.
Title: The gentrification of the internet : how to reclaim our digital
    freedom / Jessa Lingel.
Description: Oakland, California : University of California Press, [2021] |
    Includes bibliographical references and index.
Identifiers: LCCN 2020037868 (print) | LCCN 2020037869 (ebook) |
    ISBN 9780520344907 (hardback) | ISBN 9780520975705 (ebook)
Subjects: LCSH: Digital divide. | Internet—Social aspects.
Classification: LCC HM851 .L5523 2021 (print) | LCC HM851 (ebook) |
    DDC 303.48/33—dc23
LC record available at https://lccn.loc.gov/2020037868
LC ebook record available at https://lccn.loc.gov/2020037869

Manufactured in the United States of America

25 24 23 22 21
10 9 8 7 6 5 4 3 2 1

Contents

Acknowledgments   *vii*

1. Gentrification Online and Off   *1*

2. The People and Platforms Facebook Left Behind   *22*

3. The Big Problems of Big Tech   *43*

4. The Fight for Fiber   *71*

5. Resistance   *96*

List of Resources   *113*
Glossary   *121*
Sources and Further Reading   *125*
Index   *143*

Acknowledgments

In the process of writing this book, I went up for tenure, had a baby, and lived through a global pandemic. Any one of those things could easily strain the strongest support system, and yet, in a period of total exhaustion, I found constant comfort and encouragement from friends, family, colleagues, comrades, and neighbors. (Also my dog and two cats.) I'm endlessly grateful to all of these folks for their patient and insistent support.

The most direct contributions came from people who brainstormed ideas and read chapters. Early conversations with Tarleton Gillespie, Aram Sinnreich, and Siva Vaidhyanathan provided a boost in thinking this book could be a good idea. Betty Ferrari, Ben Merriman, Victor Pickard, and Aaron Shapiro read drafts of chapters, and their feedback was invaluable. Librarian warrior princess Alison Macrina read the whole damn book and gave me incredible feedback and much needed encouragement. Shane Ferrer-Sheehy, Muira McCammon, and Mariela Morales provided research assistance as the chapters came together. At the University of California Press, Lyn Uhl and Michelle Lipinski were incredibly supportive as I pitched, drafted, and revised this book.

Since moving to Philadelphia five years ago, I have connected with a number of activist groups that have shaped my relationship to the city in key ways. The Creative Resilience Collective has been an incredible source of inspiration and solidarity in its work on connecting underserved populations to resources for mental health care. 215 People's Alliance and the Workers Solidarity Network have modeled for me how people-powered groups can commit to social justice at the street and neighborhood level. The labor and agendas of these groups may not be immediately obvious in this text, but they're there in the seams and margins.

I joined the faculty at the University of Pennsylvania in 2015, and since then I've been given the time and support to teach, conduct research, and write books. I'm grateful to Penn for providing an intellectual home with wonderful colleagues, students, and staff. Yet I also recognize that the university has played a major role in the gentrification of Philadelphia—it has even given rise to the term "Penn-trification." Penn ranks sixth among U.S. universities with the largest endowments (with funds valued at over $14 billion), while Philadelphia is the country's poorest big city. As the city's largest employer and one of the country's most elite educational institutions, Penn contributes to Philadelphia's economic health and its cultural prestige. But Penn has been much more committed to scholarly research than to the wellbeing of its neighbors. Penn is one of only two Ivy League schools that do not pay property taxes to the city (Columbia being the other) and has so far resisted the call to make payments in lieu of taxes (also called PILOTs). Penn gains a lot from being in Philadelphia and should pay its fair share as a way of giving back to the city.

In addition to contributing PILOTs, Penn could demonstrate leadership around the nationwide movement to defund police.

Collectively, Penn's campus police make up the largest private police department in the state of Pennsylvania, and Penn has the third largest number of sworn police officers of universities nation-wide. Under the guise of promoting student, staff, and faculty safety, campus police can create real harm and trauma for local residents. Instead of spending $27 million on campus police, perhaps that money could be redirected to additional resources for mental health and mutual aid between the Penn community and our neighbors. A true commitment to inclusion, innovation, and impact would involve a serious reckoning with Penn's obligations to the City of Philadelphia, the neighborhoods of West Philadelphia, and the production of inequality. I hope that Penn, already a beacon of academic success and prestige, will work harder to become the kind of neighbor that Philadelphia deserves.

All royalties from this book will be donated to the Tech Learning Collective in New York City and the Women's Community Revitalization Project in Philadelphia.

1 *Gentrification Online and Off*

This is a book about technology, power, dignity, and freedom. It is about the commercialization of online platforms and the suppression of community. It is about the gentrification of the internet. When I call the internet gentrified, I'm describing shifts in power and control that limit what we can do online. I'm also calling out an industry that prioritizes corporate profits over public good and actively pushes certain forms of online behavior as the "right" way to use the web, while other forms of behavior get labeled backward or out of date. Over time, it has become harder for people to keep personal information private, to experiment or play with digital technologies, and to control how the web looks and feels. The internet is increasingly making us less democratic, more isolated, and more beholden to corporations and their shareholders. In other words, the internet has gentrified.

Gentrification is a very loaded term. It has supporters and detractors who see the world in vastly different ways. Is it helpful to use such a polarizing concept as the main argument of a book? And even if it is, is it useful to think of the internet as gentrified? I'll argue that it's precisely because the word *gentrification* is so loaded that it's a good starting point for thinking about the politics of the internet. By leaning into the conflicts around urban gentrification, we can make sense of the political realities of the internet. Gentrification gives us a metaphor for understanding how we got to the internet we have now and how it could be different.

When people connect gentrification to the internet, they're usually talking about the tech industry's role in reshaping neighborhoods that host tech company headquarters. When tech companies move their headquarters to a city or neighborhood, their workers usually follow, driving up rents and bringing new social norms. Longtime residents get pushed out and are excluded from whatever benefits tech companies might bring.

These are important problems (and I'll get to them in chapter 3), but it's not the whole story. In addition to physical spaces being warped by Big Tech, online spaces and relationships are increasingly dictated by corporations instead of being driven by communities. A small number of companies control a huge percentage of online technologies. Facebook (which also owns Instagram and WhatsApp) dominates the market for social media users, shifting a huge amount of economic and political power to one corporation. Meanwhile, Google controls online searches with a whopping 86 percent of the global market, according to the website Statista. The next most popular search engine, Bing, doesn't even come close. Amazon has redefined what online shopping looks like, predicting our interests and changing norms around the marketplace. Power is so concentrated that living without the Big Five tech companies (Amazon, Apple, Facebook, Google, and Microsoft) isn't just inconvenient, it's almost impossible. Meanwhile, another monopoly controls digital infrastructure, with a cadre of ISPs dictating who gets internet access and how much it costs.

If we look at who works in Big Tech, it's no surprise that industry priorities are skewed. Overwhelmingly run by White people and cis men, Big Tech has a tendency to ignore people of color, as well as women, people with disabilities, and LGBTQ people. And just like "urban renewal" tends to reward people who are already wealthy, innovation in Big Tech has made a lot of money for a small number of people. But there's more than just money at stake: Big Tech has fought against efforts to give more people more power, like federal regulation and employee unions. Within the industry, the biggest players have monopolized digital culture, pushing out smaller companies and older platforms. In this process of displacement, mainstream platforms get to define what online interactions are normal and what online interactions are problematic. Condensing this much control goes beyond a reduction of consumer choice; it's a form of technological gentrification.

By calling the contemporary internet gentrified, my goal is to diagnose a set of problems and lay out what activists, educators, and ordinary web users can do to carve out more protections and spaces of freedom online. The web we have wasn't inevitable. It's the result of a specific set of policies and values. Gentrification helps us understand the story of a changing internet, identifying winners and losers, and suggesting a vision for a fairer digital landscape. To start making this case, we need to be clear about gentrification. We can start by asking, What is urban gentrification and how does it help describe the modern, mainstream internet?

What Is Gentrification?

Gentrification is a loaded and controversial term. Some people think of it as an opportunity for economic development, a way to bring money and resources to poor neighborhoods. Others see an invasion of newcomers who will displace longstanding social networks and their cultural histories. Part of the problem is that gentrification isn't just one thing—instead, there are a bunch of labels and stakeholders with competing ideas about how city space should look and feel, and who should get to live there. As a starting point for understanding what gentrification means and why it matters, we can look at how urban studies scholar Gina Perez defined it:

> An economic and social process whereby private capital (real estate firms, developers) and individual homeowners and renters reinvest in fiscally neglected neighborhoods through housing rehabilitation, loft conversions, and the construction of new housing stock. . . . Gentrification is a gradual process, occurring one building or block at a time, slowly reconfiguring the neighborhood landscape of consumption and residence by displacing poor and working-class residents unable to afford to live in "revitalized" neighborhoods with rising rents, property taxes, and new businesses catering to an upscale clientele.

Gentrification involves the cooperation of developers and local governments, as well as individual homeowners and renters. It isn't just about the *presence* of newcomers, it's about their priorities. With support from local governments and financial institutions, gentrifiers transform space and remake it according to their tastes and values.

Gentrification is fundamentally about power. As urban studies scholar Sharon Zukin has written, "Gentrification makes inequality more visible." It's a contest between groups of people with different levels of power and resources. In the United States, the concept is often tied to race: gentrification usually means young, affluent, White people displace longtime residents, who are usually people of color with fewer financial resources. Racism and other kinds of discrimination have long shaped who gets to live where in the United States. Whether we're talking about redlining and biased mortgage lending or the forced relocation of Native Americans, in the United States, the freedom to live where we want has not been available to everyone. Many activists think of gentrification as yet another form of social and economic exclusion driven by bias and privilege.

Gentrification changes who lives in a neighborhood, which businesses will thrive, and who's likely to find work. In my neighborhood in South Philadelphia, I've seen locally owned bodegas, diners, and community centers turn into yoga studios, gastropubs, and brunch spots. The goal of these new businesses is not only to match the interests of newcomers but also to bring similar people to the neighborhood. If you like yoga, craft beer, and fancy French toast, these new businesses may seem pretty great. But if you can't afford to shop at the new stores or if they don't have things you want to buy, you now have to travel farther to find stores that meet your needs, your neighbors could be out of a job, and you also have highly visible reminders of who's meant to feel welcome in the neighborhood.

We often think of gentrification as something spatial, but its consequences unfold over time. More affluent neighbors raise home values and property taxes. Eventually, previously affordable neighborhoods become out of reach for families who may have lived in the neighborhood for generations. As a result, people move out, which breaks up longstanding social ties and weakens community cohesion. An irony of gentrification is that many newcomers seek out urban areas that have a strong sense of community and culture, only to threaten the very characteristics that first drew them to the neighborhood.

Since at least the 1960s, researchers have tracked gentrification across the globe. For most of human history, people lived in rural or semirural areas, and cities were often viewed as hotspots of crime and pollution. While many people still think of cities as dirty and crime-ridden, as of 2014, more people in the world live in urban areas than not, according to a report from the United Nations. Cities have always been associated with economic growth and cultural invention, but what's new to the twenty-first century is how many wealthy people are choosing to live in urban environments. For example, in 2019, *US News* announced that San Francisco became the city with the most billionaires per capita— one for every 11,612 people. Gentrification advocates like to point out that wealthy neighbors pay higher property taxes (which isn't true in cities that give gentrifiers tax breaks or abatements). But a sudden increase in wealthy neighbors also has negative consequences. Rich newcomers can push out longtime residents by physically taking up more space, as houses that used to accommodate multiple families are turned into mansions for single families. Even more damaging are so-called investment properties, which are purchased by people who have no intention of living there. Betting that the appeal of urban living will continue, investors purchase houses and apartments in the same way that people speculate on art or gold. A journalist for the *Guardian*, Tracey Lindeman, has been tracking investment properties in major Canadian cities. In Vancouver, twenty-five thousand properties (about 10 percent of the total) are unoccupied, most of which are investment properties. On the other side of Canada, almost 40 percent of Toronto's condos are unoccupied or short-term rentals. This is despite a fierce demand for affordable housing in both cities. From Oakland to Baltimore, Sao Paulo to Amsterdam, and Istanbul to Sydney, people are struggling to find affordable housing.

People who see gentrification as a good thing tend to emphasize opportunities for new businesses and real estate development. But these benefits aren't evenly distributed. Urban gentrification has a tendency to make rich people richer and poor people poorer. According to a *Guardian* special report on crime and gentrification, for each millionaire household in the San Francisco Bay Area (and there are more than two hundred thousand), there are four new people living below the poverty level. Newcomers may think they're improving the neighborhood, but what improvement means depends on your priorities—and whether you can afford to stay in a neighborhood where the cost of housing is on the rise.

Gentrification changes the physical spaces in a neighborhood, bringing different architectural aesthetics and new kinds of businesses. Over time, existing houses seem smaller and more dated, and old businesses lose customers as new residents bring demands for cosmopolitan perks. Gentrification also changes the social norms in a neighborhood, with the potential for clashes over noise, parenting styles, and even pets.

Who's responsible for gentrification? Gentrification is a partnership between people, policymakers, and real estate companies. When we hear the word *gentrifier,* we might think of young, White couples moving into a neighborhood, looking for affordable housing in urban areas. Young people are increasingly eager to start their careers and families in cities, and empty nesters are moving to cities rather than staying in the suburbs. But it's also important to realize that gentrification isn't just about personal decisions about where to live or individual landlords bumping up the rent for tenants. At the city level, gentrification involves tax breaks for new construction and sometimes more drastic approaches, like eminent domain, which means the city takes over one or more properties to build a new development or expand infrastructure. (I'll get into local policies meant to kickstart gentrification, like those enacted by local governments trying to attract Big Tech companies to their cities, in chapter 3).

Local policies are one piece of the puzzle, but another key force is the banking and real estate industry. In some cases, bankers, realtors, and landlords will deliberately exclude people from real estate opportunities based on prejudice. Called redlining, this practice systematically excludes people of color (and historically, other groups, like unmarried women and Jewish people) from owning property. In the United States, redlining was finally outlawed in the 1970s, but the problem has been difficult to stamp out. The Department of Housing and Urban Development (HUD) announced a $200 million settlement with Associated Bank over redlining in Chicago and Milwaukee in May 2015. A three-year HUD investigation found that the Associated Bank purposely rejected mortgage applications from Black and Latinx applicants. Others have noted that the risky mortgage lending at the root of the 2008 financial recession also discriminated against the poor and people of color, with banks deliberately targeting these groups as customers for predatory lending agreements. The wave of foreclosures that followed fueled house-flipping across the country. Investors and developers scooped up foreclosed houses, setting off new waves of gentrification in neighborhoods that were already hard-hit.

Gentrification has become a money-making strategy implemented by megafirms with Wall Street backing. Ben Lane, a journalist for the real estate publication *HousingWire,* has docu-mented a powerful shift in landlords in the United States. In 2017, the rental company Invitation Homes merged with Starwood Waypoint Homes, creating the nation's largest landlord, with roughly eighty-two thousand homes across the country. Another Wall Street–backed firm, American Homes 4 Rent, owns forty-nine thousand homes in twenty-two states. When Wall Street sets the terms of a rental agreement, what kind of landlord do you get? For many renters of single-family homes, the answer is a landlord who doesn't make repairs or exceptions for late payments. A report from the Federal Reserve Bank of Atlanta found that corporate owners of single-family rental homes were more likely than smaller landlords to evict tenants; some filed eviction notices on a third of their renters in just one year. As difficult as it might be to convince your upstairs landlord to fix a sink or accept a late payment, nego-tiating with a major corporate lender can be even more futile. In 2020, COVID-19 exposed how vulnerable renters are during finan-cial and health crises: while housing advocates and activists demanded universal rent relief and a moratorium on evictions, local and state governments were able to protect only renters living in federally backed housing.

Urban studies researchers have been writing about gentrifica-tion for over fifty years, and not everyone describes it in the same way or focuses on the same politics. If we're not precise about what the word *gentrification* means, then all we have is the anger and confusion associated with it. To use the concept to think about the internet, it's important to be really clear about what I mean when I use the word *gentrification* in this book. Here are the key features of urban gentrification to keep in mind before we start applying the concept to the internet:

Gentrification involves displacement. Over time, longstanding communities and their histories get pushed out to make way for newcomers.

Gentrification is about power.

Gentrification takes more than a handful of people moving into a neighborhood; it also requires the support of local financial and legal systems.

Gentrification is a process that gets active help from local laws and rules that offer tax breaks to developers and from city officials who actively call for real estate investment.

Gentrification has to do with homes as well as businesses. The residential side of gentrification involves the replacement of one community with another, but the business side can be just as important in terms of local employment opportunities.

Gentrification can't be fought on an individual level; it takes a community. Because gentrification is bigger than a handful of people, houses, or businesses, challenging it has to combine individual practices with collective action and new regulations.

How Is the Internet Gentrifying?

Now that we have a clear sense of what gentrification means, we can start to think about how key themes of gentrification show up online. Across different cities and neighborhoods, gentrification exaggerates inequality and normalizes certain social values while excluding others. Something similar has happened to the internet. A growing number of journalists, lawmakers, activists, and tech insiders have raised concerns about discrimination, segregation, and commercialization online. The techno-optimism that defined the 1990s and early 2000s has faded, and many of us are left wondering how we could have ever believed that the web would deliver on promises of democracy and equality. Once we get past these rather utopian hopes, however, we can begin thinking more critically about the internet and its politics. What kinds of communities and norms are actively promoted on the mainstream web? Who's making it rich in Big Tech? Who's being left behind? What are the rules and regulations that could skew power in a different way? Keeping theories of gentrification in mind, I see three key characteristics of gentrification in the contemporary web, all of which limit online freedoms for individuals in order to support the interests of major tech companies.

Displacement

Gentrification happens when there's a transition of people and power. The LA Tenants Union brings together local activists committed to pushing back against gentrification. According to the group's cofounder, Tracy Jeanne Rosenthal, we should think of gentrification as "displacement and replacement of the poor for profit." This process tends to unfold slowly. Gradually, new neighbors raise property values and taxes. Rising costs make neighborhoods unaffordable for their original residents, and for people of the same demographic. Social ties have more power when they have history, and gentrification threatens existing social ties and erases local histories. People move. Streets, neighborhoods, and landmarks get renamed. Businesses that sustained a community are bought out and remade to attract new customers. Online, gentrification happens as older platforms struggle to compete with the resources and values of newer platforms. For communities that have been online a long time, competing with new platforms like

Facebook and Instagram becomes a losing battle as they are out-spent and out-coded by the seemingly endless resources of Big Tech. The result is less creativity and diversity as far as the kinds of platforms that get major investment. The risk here is that platforms and their communities will be left behind, not because they've stopped working but because they've stopped looking or feeling like the rest of the web. We're left with platforms that are less inclusive. The result isn't just that *who's* online has changed, it's that *what's* online is more likely to be biased, disempowering, or just plain old boring.

Isolation

Over time, gentrification results in pockets of isolation where long-time residents are boxed in by new neighbors who are often wealthier and have different ideas about who and what belongs in the neighborhood. Neighbors can wind up deeply segregated, living next door but going to different churches, sending their kids to different schools, and shopping at different stores. We can compare this to how users online get labeled and sorted by mainstream platforms. Before social media, forming communities online mostly meant meeting new people with a shared interest, which could be anything from Star Trek to hip hop to soccer. Early on, there were no algorithms for categorizing users, no platform-based recommendations of friends or content. People just showed up at a message board or in a chatroom and hung out with whoever was around. (Of course, who showed up was driven largely by who could afford a modem and had the time to learn how to use it.) Platforms like Reddit and 4chan still operate this way, but most social media platforms use existing IRL personal networks to link users and push content. Over time, it's become the norm for platforms to suggest links and videos based on users' likes and personal affinity, which creates what Eli Pariser has called "filter bubbles." Watching a YouTube video on punk rock brings you to a long stream of videos that are also about punk, rather than videos about ska, rockabilly, or riot grrl. Liking a Facebook post that sees climate change as a hoax will bring up additional posts denying climate change. Rather than being exposed to diverse people and content, users are increasingly segregated and filter-bubbled. Of course, the internet didn't invent filter bubbles. As internet studies researcher Axel Bruns has argued, people have always formed into groups based on ideas. Immigrant newspapers, religious radio stations, hobby club newsletters—people have always created sources of community and media to reflect their ideas and values. More than just creating affinity links, filter bubbles can amplify the tendency for people with the same values to stick together rather than confronting new ideas. What's really troubling about online isolation is that offline, people are already siloed in terms of their social networks, meaning we tend to have friends from the same racial and class background as ourselves. The promise of early online communities was that they would get us outside those bubbles, a possibility that mainstream social media platforms increasingly limit.

Commercialization

People often defend gentrification in economic terms, emphasizing business opportunities and higher tax revenues. If all you care about is tax dollars, neighborhood newcomers with more money are more valuable as residents. Businesses and city officials justify their support of gentrification by pointing to the increase in city funds from new residents with higher tax bases. Boosted by the approval of realtors and local officials, gentrifiers may feel more entitled to claim space and assert their preferences. What drops out of these calculations are social and cultural values, like community ties and local histories. Focusing solely on profits is a very narrow way of deciding what's best for a neighborhood. Gentrification isn't about introducing commercialism to a neighborhood for the first time, it's about catering to specific kinds of consumers and businesses. Commercial properties in gentrified neighborhoods are often incredibly monotonous. As Kevin Baker, a journalist writing about gentrification in New York City, observed, "Chain stores, of a type once unknown in New York, now abound. On those same ten blocks of my neighborhood where so many stores have been emptied out, I count three pharmacies, six bank branches, seven nail-and-beauty salons, three Starbucks, two Dunkin' Donuts and three 7-Elevens, five phone-and-cable stores, four eyewear shops. The coming growth industry seems to be in urgent care facilities, of which there are already two, to serve our ridiculously underinsured population."

Despite the sameness of the stores and shops themselves, commercial opportunities become a key justification for supporting gentrification. Similarly, the tech industry tends to defend itself by pointing to profits. Why does Facebook sell our personal data to advertisers? Profits. Why doesn't Amazon treat its employees better or let them unionize? Profits. Why don't tech companies do more to protect privacy? Profits. It's maximizing profits that determines whether a tech company is successful. As long as Big Tech sees itself as more accountable to shareholders than users, the ability of ordinary people to demand changes will be limited.

Throughout this book, I'll come back to the themes of displacement, isolation, and commercialization as a guide for understanding the gentrification of the internet. These characteristics act as signposts or building blocks for reading the politics of Big Tech, and for thinking critically about how we got to the web we have now and how it could be different. Activist organizers use digital technology to communicate, plan events, and push for change. Relying on these tools for organizing doesn't mean we can't ask tough questions about this tech. We need more frameworks that can help identify adversaries in the struggle for more ethical technology *and* more ethical cities. I'm putting gentrification out there as just this kind of framework. In the next four chapters, I make the case that the internet is gentrifying, which we can see in digital culture, the tech industry, and digital infrastructure. Thinking about gentrification is a starting point in finding our way to a less commercial, more diverse internet.

You may have your doubts about using the term *gentrification* to describe the internet. I can imagine skeptical readers asking: *Was the internet ever really ungentrified?* The short answer is, no. There was no golden age when the internet was blind to race, class, and gender, no magical era when communities could thrive without corporate interference and a push toward profits. Histories of the internet show us that the U.S. military was key to building the internet and that corporations have always shaped the internet's look and feel. I don't want to romanticize the early web as a paradise of rambunctious hackers and quirky tinkerers, and I also don't want to paint a one-sided picture where all tech companies are evil. The transitions I'm describing are about major trends within the tech industry and digital culture. And there's no denying that a small number of high-powered corporations have come to have significant control over what the web looks and feels like. The internet's early emphasis on invention and creativity has largely been displaced by corporate profiteering. Just like urban gentrification, it's not the existence of tech companies that creates a gentrified internet, it's the use of commercial profits to justify decisions that benefit the few at the expense of the many. The fact that a neighborhood is gentrifying doesn't mean that it used to be perfect and now it's a prison or a wasteland. It means that as a whole, it's become harder for some groups of people to thrive and easier for some groups to get ahead.

Do we really need the word gentrification *to talk about this? Aren't you just talking about capitalism?* Yes, the forces of gentrification are very much wrapped up in capitalism, and it's difficult to criticize one without criticizing the other. I focus on gentrification because I want to address the race, gender, and class politics involved in how the internet has transformed over time. Terms like *commercialized, capitalist,* and *corporate* are all related to the process I'm calling gentrification, but they don't do enough to pull in connections to race, gender, and class. Gentrification is also a very spatial concept, which can make it feel more concrete than capitalism. As a word that makes us think about houses, streets, and rent, gentrification helps us consider who feels at home on mainstream platforms and who gets left out, who gets to see themselves and their politics represented and who gets ignored.

Urban gentrification is a process of physical movement; how can the same thing happen online? For one thing, I'll argue in chapter 3 that the tech industry contributes directly to urban gentrification. And in chapter 4, I'll show how online gentrification involves the control of physical objects like cable and fiber. But I agree that there's a key difference between the movement of people online versus in city space. After all, neighborhoods only have space for so many people, but Facebook can sign up as many members as it wants. Currently, about one third of the world's inhabitants have a Facebook account, more than the population of any individual country or religion. Urban gentrification isn't just about newcomers showing up in a neighborhood, it's about people who are forced to leave because they no longer feel welcome—or can't afford to stay. A gentrifying internet doesn't force people to pack up their stuff and move house. But it does mean people online are being resituated and homogenized in ways that usually don't serve the community's particular needs or values.

Any metaphor can be stretched too far or taken too literally, at which point it becomes confusing or misleading instead of being helpful. A metaphor is only as valuable as its analytical payoff, meaning that it is useful as long as it helps us to think about a phenomenon in a new way. In the following chapters, I'll show how gentrification gives us a vocabulary for thinking about the internet's politics and inequalities. In terms of how ordinary people experience the internet, the past few decades have seen a transition from messy serendipity and DIY communities to slick professionalism and algorithmic sorting. These changes have consequences that affect what kinds of communities we can build online. And the changes I'm talking about aren't random—they're the result of a specific set of goals and policies. Like urban gentrification, development of digital culture supports the needs and tastes of a wealthy minority. Gentrification shows us winners, losers, and subversives in the current digital landscape.

This book comes from years of thinking about and researching the internet in everyday life. I've been teaching courses on technology and culture for a decade, and I've noticed a major change in my students' assumptions about the internet. In 2010, students mostly saw the internet and social media as Good Things. Before Edward Snowden revealed the scale of government surveillance, before the Cambridge Analytica scandal broke, and before concerns around fake news on social media grew rampant, my students connected the internet to innovation and financial success, to democracy and social inclusion. Ten years later, students bring a very different set of assumptions to class. They tend to see the internet as a source of surveillance and discrimination, as something that offers a lot of conveniences, but which come at a major cost. I used to see my job as teaching students how to think about hidden power dynamics online. A decade ago, I had to work pretty hard to convince students that the internet came with very real harms, particularly for marginalized groups. Now, my students come to class assuming that online content can be fake, manipulative, and monitored, and my goal is to explain how we got to the web we have and how it could be different. Over the next four chapters, I will show how gentrification theory is one part of a toolkit for understanding how the online landscape came to be what it is and offer some ideas on how we can get the web we want.

I mentioned earlier that urban gentrification is a global phenomenon. Across the world, more and more people are moving to cities, and as they do, more and more inequality is taking hold. Similarly, gentrification applies to technologies across the globe, with displacement, isolation, and commercialization popping up on an international set of platforms. To keep this book focused and its ideas manageable, most of my examples will come from the United States. The decisions and factors that lead to gentrification can have an international reach, but their roots are local, based in local politics and industry norms. By focusing on policies and industries in the United States, I can get specific about how online gentrification happens as a result of particular priorities and stakeholders. My hope is that gentrification can be a framework that crosses different borders and divides, but I don't want to imply that the internet is the same everywhere or that the U.S. tech industry is the only one that matters. Hopefully, other researchers and activists can try out this framework in new spaces and contexts to make sense of the power dynamics at stake for other sets of people and platforms.

This is a good point to be clear about who this book is for. I'm not writing this book for other researchers who study the internet. I've written two longer, denser books about the politics of digital technologies that are geared toward academics. With this book, I'm trying to reach a different group of readers: activists and ordinary internet users who want to think critically about the internet. A lot of academic work has helped me develop these ideas, but I've tried to clear out most of the academic jargon and also avoid citations and footnotes because I want this book to be accessible to people outside the academy. There's a glossary of key terms at the end of the book to help readers keep track of special vocabulary. There's also a list of references so that interested readers can learn more about these topics.

To understand how we got to a point of reduced freedom and increased commercialization online, we have to think about the different components that make up the internet. These include the norms of social media platforms where we spend time online, the businesses that create digital tools and services, and the physical infrastructure that makes the internet possible. In the next three chapters, I describe how these different features—culture, industry, and infrastructure—have gentrified. I've spent years studying online communities and technological change, particularly among marginalized groups. I'll bring these stories into my discussion of online gentrification as a way of showing how changing norms and politics play out for real communities and users. In the final chapter, I describe potential paths of resistance, inspired by urban activists fighting back against local gentrification.

Finally, before I get any further into a book that uses gentrification as its central concept, I want to own the fact that I've contributed to many of the processes that I'm critiquing in this book. I'm a White, cis, college-educated woman, and between spending my twenties in Brooklyn and my midthirties in Philadelphia, most of my addresses over the past fifteen years have included zip codes of some of the country's most rapidly gentrifying neighborhoods. I currently live in a historically Black neighborhood in South Philadelphia, and in many ways, this book comes from thinking about my role in gentrification. While I can choose not to go to the yoga studio or the brunch bistro that have opened up near my house since I moved in, I know these businesses are targeting people like me as customers. I can choose not to buy a house that's been flipped and to opt out of a tax abatement, but my living in the neighborhood still makes it more likely that people who look like me will buy property in the area.

By using gentrification as a metaphor for understanding online politics and technological ethics, I don't mean to downplay urban gentrification as an important social issue. Trying to come to terms with my role in gentrification has helped me to be a better activist, and it's also helped me think of the internet in a new way. I've thought a lot about what it means to be a good neighbor and the ways that my presence affects the lives of the people around me. Getting involved with gentrification activists in Philadelphia has helped me to understand the need to preserve a neighborhood's history and culture, and how much work it takes to fight back against lawmakers and developers who look at a neighborhood like mine and see only dollar signs. Mostly, I've spent a lot of time listening: going to local zoning meetings to hear how neighbors feel about new houses and businesses, and showing up to hear city council representatives talk about their housing policies. The conversations at zoning meetings and activist meetups are so different from those I have when I talk to people who are new to the neighborhood. Realtors use words like "pioneering," while activists talk about "invasion." Developers talk about "revitalization," while longtime residents say things like "disrespecting our communities." In some ways, it's the gap between these two sides that makes gentrification such an important word for thinking about the internet. It's a word that lays out two very different sets of values and assumptions, which can help us think more clearly about the politics and possibilities of digital technologies.

2 The People and Platforms Facebook Left Behind

Whether online or off, gentrification raises the same questions about community and privilege: Who's being actively invited into a space, and who's being pushed out? Who benefits from new businesses, new social norms, and new rules, and who loses? Who gets a seat at the table, and who gets left behind? The key features of urban gentrification that I pointed out in the last chapter—commercialization, isolation, and displacement—all have online counterparts. In the links between urban and online gentrification, we see power struggles around accessing resources, expressing identity, and the ability of communities to grow and thrive.

Digital platforms welcome some groups more than others. As big platforms get bigger, smaller platforms get left behind. As a result, online experiences become less diverse and more predictable, less open and more exploitative. There are two ways that digital culture can gentrify: by creating inequality between platforms and by creating inequality within platforms. The first is about displacement, or when a platform (and its politics and aesthetics) comes to dominate the online landscape, displacing competing platforms. The second is about commercialized discrimination, which happens when a platform sets up preferences that reward some groups of users over others. As an example of gentrified digital displacement, I'll describe how two online platforms—Tumblr and BME, an online community for body modification enthusiasts—each struggled to hold their own as mainstream platforms set up shop. To help us think about commercialized discrimination, I'll get into algorithmic sorting and digital redlining, which is when online advertising discriminates against users based on race and class. Each of these threads has something to teach us about how digital culture is changing. While change is inevitable when it comes to relationships between people and technology, the trend that's taken hold is one of increased commercial power and decreased people power. Understanding how we got here is a crucial first step for asking, Is this the web we want? And if not, how can we make it different?

RIP Early Internet: Revisiting a Weirder and More Open Web

Facebook, Instagram, YouTube—these platforms have gotten so big that they feel like mega big-box stores. It wasn't always this way. In its early days, the web looked less like a mall full of big-box stores and more like a flea market full of side hustles. Anyone with basic html skills could have a web presence and reach a niche audience. Before social media platforms, browsing the web could be confusing and slow, but it was also weird and surprising. People set up web pages devoted to their pet cats, obscure kinds of music, or TV shows. Others created LGBTQ support networks and forums dedicated to mental health or political organizing. There was a lot of experimentation and silliness, as well as difficult questions about how to sustain communities and maintain order. Over time, new platforms emerged that required fewer skills to use—instead of needing to know html, users could post, upload, and connect with minimal know-how. The barrier to entry got a lot lower, but it came at the cost of less openness and more commercial priorities for platforms. As big platforms got even larger, they left behind online communities that couldn't keep up with the demand for sophisticated tech and bigger audiences.

In any industry, businesses come and go. Bebo, Formspring, Friendster, PlanetAll, StumbleUpon—at one point, each of these platforms had millions of users. Now they're all defunct. Why should we care if Bebo and Friendster didn't make the cut? Historians of technology often find it more useful to look at failures than successes because technologies that seemed promising but then died off can reveal alternate paths. Like big-box stores and chain stores, the biggest platforms prioritize the average and ignore outliers. But if we look to the edges of the web, at platforms that failed or never made it big, we see new possibilities for digital tech. If we hear only about the biggest companies, we get only their vision of how the internet came to be. If we want the whole story, we have to learn about the people and platforms with different ideas about the internet's histories and values.

As a researcher, most of my work investigates people on the margins and their relationships to technology. Drag queens, punk rockers, people with extreme body modification—I've spent months, and in some cases years, with these countercultural groups to learn how they make sense of the internet. Many of these communities have struggled to make the internet meet their needs. Much like activists, countercultural groups have their own ideas about how to use digital technology for building community and self-expression. If you're a drag queen, you might want more flexibility around user names and the ability to have multiple accounts on one site. If you're into extreme genital piercings, you need looser rules around censorship of digital content. And if you're running an underground music scene, you'll have questions about whether the police have access to your community's online content. Some countercultural groups use mainstream platforms, finding hacks and workarounds to make social media meet their needs. Other communities build their own platforms to have full control over policies for users and site design. For a closer look at the gap between what countercultural groups want and what mainstream platforms have, we can look at BME, short for Body Modification E-Zine.

BME got its start in 1994, back in the web's early days and ten years before students at Harvard were sending the first pokes and friend requests on Facebook. BME brought together an international group of body modification enthusiasts, which included people interested in tattoos and piercings, plus more unusual practices like scarification, suspensions and flesh pulls, corseting, ear pointing, tongue splitting, extreme genital modifications, and the voluntary amputation of digits, limbs, and organs. Over the next two decades, BME would become a vibrant source of community and the primary online resource for information about body modification. It would also act as a countercultural canary in the coal mine of social media gentrification.

From the start, BME saw itself as an online haven for people on the margins. Its front-page statement of purpose laid out its countercultural agenda: "We are an uncommon subculture and community built by and for modified people. We are the historians, practitioners and appreciators of body modification. We are the collaborative and comprehensive resource for the freedom of individuality in thought, expression and aesthetic. We serve you and ourselves as a source of inspiration, entertainment and community. There are still tons of different platforms online, catering to every possible group, subculture and community." BME was created as a community-based platform, geared toward people who shared an interest in body modification. As one BME member that I interviewed in 2014 explained, "Essentially I see BME as a social network for people of the industry or people interested in the industry. Everyone that follows the culture and life of tattoos and piercing."

When BME got its start in the 1990s, both the internet and body modification were countercultural. BME predates social media giants like Facebook and Twitter, as well as online staples like Google and WordPress. Digital culture was still up for grabs, meaning BME could experiment with norms and business models for online communities. Fewer people were online, and there was less conformity in the rules for good and bad behavior on the internet. For most of its history, BME was built by members of the community, so its policies and design came from body modification insiders rather than the tech industry. BME followed the model of early internet chatrooms, bringing people together based on a topic. Now, Facebook hosts groups based on interests and experiences, from manga to MAGA and cancer survivors to women's soccer. But the original idea behind Facebook was always to link people who share an IRL connection. On BME, like most early internet groups, a common interest came first, and building relationships followed. While extreme forms of body modification are still rare, now-common modifications like piercings and tattoos were more stigmatized thirty years ago. Folks with more extreme modifications were most drawn to BME as a source of community. The site's founder, Shannon Larratt, was passionately curious about cutting-edge body modification procedures like eyeball tattooing and radical genital modification. Technologically and culturally, BME was at the forefront, and its battle for success and survival anticipated a broader struggle for authenticity online.

From a high point in the early 2000s of around ten thousand users and hundreds of daily interactions, BME's membership had dwindled to a few dozen active users by 2015. Forums and message boards that used to see hundreds of post a day now go months without an update. What happened? BME survived many twists and turns in digital culture, evolving from a Bulletin Board System (BBS) to an Internet Relay Chat (IRC) to a stand-alone platform. But its biggest challenge wasn't so much technological as social. A couple of factors led to a steep decline in use and membership. First, BME administrators launched a site redesign in 2011. A private company was hired, and for the first time, the platform was rebuilt by community outsiders. Over budget, repeatedly delayed, and poorly communicated to users, the redesign ultimately alienated many longtime BME members. At the same time, changing norms around self-promotion and chasing likes clashed with BME's vibe of exclusivity. Platforms like Facebook and Instagram promised audiences that went beyond a niche community. Posts that could get a dozen likes on BME could get tens of thousands on Facebook. Sensing the shifting tides, BME's administrators began pleading with users to post body modification content to BME first and other platforms later. But over time, more and more BME members opened up accounts on Facebook, posting less and less to BME. User engagement dropped, and Facebook's membership climbed. BME struggled not because people were no longer interested in body modification but because people wanted to share their experiences with as many people as possible.

Communities on the margins are constantly at risk of being displaced by mainstream platforms. BME's struggle for survival shows us how hard it is for smaller platforms to compete with mainstream giants. There are now far more BME users on Facebook than on BME—Facebook has two user groups exclusively for former BME members. If they're still able to connect online, what do BME users lose by transitioning to Facebook? Facebook has the same advantages of digital connection, plus more features, mostly bug-free design, and a much, much larger user base. But BME users on Facebook have to follow Facebook's rules, which means that body modification photos are regularly flagged as inappropriate. (BME Hard, a members-only photo gallery of bondage, sadomasochism, and genital modification photos, could never operate on Facebook.) BME also provided more privacy for people interested in extreme procedures, which ran the risk of social stigmatization and sometimes skirted the law. On Facebook, body modification enthusiasts have to conform to more bougie, uptight values. Instead of being "an uncommon subculture and community built by and for modified people," BME is now fractured, and the community is ultimately governed by "normies" and "plainskins," as BME folks sometimes call people without piercings and tattoos.

I first started thinking about online gentrification based on a conversation with Rachel Larratt, who took over BME in 2011. Having been involved with BME almost from the beginning, Rachel had experienced firsthand the challenges of trying to keep a small online platform in the black. She had also seen changes in digital culture up close. In a 2016 interview, I asked Rachel about whether Facebook could be a home for a community like BME. Her response was not optimistic:

They [Facebook] don't want to be like, "Hey we are just an online forum that the people use." They are trying to foster that idea [of community]. It's just staged, like a really big-box store trying pretend like they are a local small business owner. The reason why I'm saying I don't like BME [being on] Facebook is because it's, again, it's supporting a "community," in quotes, but does not support *our* community. It's crazy because the only people making money off of those groups are Facebook for the ad content. . . . I've always said that, like, Facebook is the Walmart of the Internet, and that Facebook came to town and just put out of business all of these smaller niche sites.

In Rachel's view, the digital landscape used to look more like a downtown with mom-and-pop businesses. Now it's mostly strip malls and big-box stores. Just as local businesses get displaced when a neighborhood gentrifies, smaller and niche platforms struggle to survive in a web dominated by major tech companies.

Another platform with a story to tell about gentrifying digital culture is Tumblr. Part microblog, part photo-sharing platform, Tumblr was created by web developers David Karp and Marco Arment and launched in 2007. Tumblr is a blogging platform for sharing videos, photos, links, and text. More media rich than microblogs like Twitter and more interactive than platforms like WordPress, Tumblr pitched itself as a community for creativity. Unlike many of its peers, Tumblr gives users a lot of flexibility to customize the appearance of user pages and profiles. On Facebook, users choose what to post and share, but the structure of a profile or page is tightly controlled by the platform. On Tumblr, users can have multiple profiles without breaking user guidelines. They can also change the look and feel of their profiles and pages, and edit the html of their posts. With loose rules on censorship and an emphasis on inclusion, Tumblr became a haven for queer and trans people. The platform also hosted a vibrant network of users who posted not safe for work (NSFW) content. This included erotic art, poetry, fiction, and (especially) photography. In a study on Tumblr's asexual community, Bryce Renninger argued that several features made Tumblr attractive for people on the margins: trolling is disincentivized, posts are easily traced back to the original poster (OP, in Tumblr-speak), privacy and anonymity are allowed, and a user's status (the number of followers or length of time on the platform) is de-emphasized. These features made for a cabaret-like vibe on the platform, where users felt free to express themselves and find likeminded people without worrying too much about platform oversight.

Riding a wave of popularity, particularly among young people, Tumblr was bought by Yahoo! in June 2013 for a whopping $1.1 billion. In 2019, it was sold to Automattic Inc., the company that owns WordPress, for just $3 million, a fraction of its previous value. What happened? How did Tumblr's value fall so far so fast? Partly, Tumblr's drop in popularity followed a familiar script of the rise and fall of social media platforms. In between 2013 and 2019, Instagram, Vine, and TikTok started to eat into Tumblr's user base. Right at the moment that Tumblr needed to set itself apart from its competitors, the platform rolled out policy changes that isolated users who had been the core of its user base. In 2018, Tumblr banned multiple categories of adult content, including "photos, videos, or GIFs" displaying explicit material, as well as "illustrations that [depict] sex acts." Suddenly, the groups that had felt most at home on Tumblr were being evicted. The new rules set off a debate over what—and who—Tumblr was for.

Users were outraged over what they saw as a betrayal of Tumblr's core values. Many accused Tumblr of going back on its commitment to safe spaces for marginalized communities. Nerd icon and Tumblr royalty Wil Wheaton weighed in on the controversy, arguing, "According to marginalized and vulnerable people, this change in policy will directly hurt them. And that's indefensible." If policy changes reflect corporate priorities, Tumblr's #NSFW and porn ban signaled a push to the mainstream. The new goal seemed to be growing its user base rather than meeting the needs of its most devoted users. As Aja Romano, a journalist at *Vox,* noted, "What's at issue is not only the question of whether Tumblr can survive its own purge but the question of who Tumblr's core users are, and what will motivate them to continue building their communities on a platform that seems to be devaluing them and their vital contributions to building Tumblr culture."

By pushing new values instead of respecting existing ones, Tumblr lost a key part of its base. Users who stuck around got a certain sense of satisfaction from the very public freefall of Tumblr's trading value. As a Tumblr user named snakegay explained in a post,

everyone who buys tumblr fundamentally misunderstands the fact that us clowns that still use this site use it specifically because its a no mans land in here and its structure utterly prevents a lot of the annoying crap on other social media. no premium nonsense, posts are in order, significant anonymity, etc. the userbase is uniquely hostile to change and will get up in arms about literally anything you do. every corporation who buys this site with different goals in mind is gonna have a bad time and end up selling it a few years down the line for chump change.

Rather than seeing users as eyeballs for an endless wheel of content, this Tumblr holdout sees people as having serious power over platforms. If users value things like "no premium nonsense, posts [being] in order, significant anonymity," they can protect these features by holding their online attention hostage. The difference here is between corporate values, based entirely on dollars and share prices, and user values, like self-expression, diversity, and anonymity.

One way of describing Tumblr's transformation from internet cool kid to abandoned ghost town is as a failed bid at gentrification. Like eager developers who wanted to take over a neighborhood, Tumblr's ownership put growth over preserving existing culture. When new residents failed to show up, those users who were left remained partly pissed off and partly relieved. As a Tumblr user named lesbianrey explained, "mandatory disclosure that i do think this site sucks but . . . tumblr's kinda nice in that its less like . . . public facing than twitter fb insta etc? more like how the Old Internet used to be where u had your own little niches . . . idk i feel like that's harder to find now." Hostile to change and willing to call out corporate leadership, some Tumblr users see value in staying on a platform that feels abandoned by the mainstream. For others, Tumblr has lost a vital part of its identity, with policies that continue to disenfranchise people on the margins.

Was Tumblr's decline inevitable? Tumblr could have leaned in to the dynamic of being a platform for queer and countercultural communities. It could have experimented with business models that didn't require hustling for the biggest possible audience. Instead, Tumblr sided with mainstream users, values, and business models. The result was financial disaster and an increasingly ambivalent user base.

Tumblr and BME represent an older ethic of digital culture. These are platforms that believed that the internet should be weird, that it's okay for people to be anonymous online, and that community is more about people than profits. The story of BME demonstrates a battle between platforms, where a small, niche site struggled to compete with a much larger platform with nearly endless resources. While BME worked to maintain its policies and stay countercultural, Tumblr sold out its base in a bid to gain more users. The result was a dramatic drop in value and a crisis of identity. Both sites lost out in the race to keep up with bigger platforms with more resources and fewer commitments to the margins. Their declines were partly the result of decisions made by the platforms themselves, which often went against the values of users who liked having an online refuge that was countercultural and diverse. In both cases, users wound up with more rules and restrictions as previously open forums for expression were transformed into less weird, more homogenous platforms that could better compete with Facebook. The rise and fall of BME and Tumblr show us what we stand to lose as norms of digital culture skew to the mainstream.

Algorithms and the Battle over "Real" Names

Big Tech platforms cater to the middle, because the margins tend to be controversial and unruly. This preference for the lowest common denominator leads to communities that are more isolated and less diverse. One key driver for making online communities feel more homogenous are the algorithms pushing content to users. Facebook's interface might look the same from one user to another, but the platform actually pushes different content to people based on past behavior. A conservative Christian and a radical pro-Palestine activist might get very different results when they Google issues related to the Middle East. Of course, the offline world has its own filter bubbles. Sociologists have found that even when people say they'd prefer to live in diverse communities, their neighborhoods often end up segregated anyway. This is what makes online isolation so depressing. The promise of early digital communities was that they would get us outside of the filter bubbles of school, work, and worship. Pushing back on IRL filter bubbles is a potential benefit of online communities that mainstream social media platforms increasingly deprioritize.

Finding ways to desegregate and deisolate is more important than ever. In the United States, schools have historically been a key battleground of segregation. Despite landmark civil rights legislation in the 1960s, racial and economic segregation in U.S. schools has been creeping upward since the 2000s. In 2016, the U.S. Government Accountability Office found that between 2000 and 2014, both the percentage of K-12 public schools classified as high-poverty and the percentage of these schools made up of mostly African American or Hispanic students grew significantly, more than doubling from 7,009 to 15,089 schools. Economic diversity is shrinking, with rich kids and poor kids increasingly attending separate schools. The percentage of schools with racial or socioeconomic isolation (schools in which 75 percent or more of students are of the same race or class) grew from 9 percent to 16 percent between 2000 and 2014. Schools are a crucial institution for shaking up our social networks and battling inequality. If our places of worship and employment are already segregated, spaces where we have the opportunity to learn different viewpoints and values become even more important. Social media platforms could help diversify our social networks. Instead, many of them push us to be more isolated.

Part of what's driving the sameness of filter bubbles is the insistence on using real names on online platforms. Trolling, flaming, fraud—we often associate bad behavior on the web with anonymity. Yet in the internet's early days, it was common to use handles, screennames, and pseudonyms. People had a lot of control over how much information existed about themselves online, and unmasking someone's identity usually required a lot of work or a depth of knowledge about their online habits. BME and Tumblr have different policies on user identity, but they both allow or encourage pseudonyms or anonymity. This is increasingly not the norm. As internet studies researcher danah boyd has pointed out, it used to be that online, you were anonymous by default and public through effort. Now, our information is out in the digital public by default, while retaining our privacy takes effort.

Why do "real" name policies matter? And how have they been challenged? In 2014, Facebook found itself battling drag queens over its real name policy. Over two hundred accounts of drag queens were reported and frozen because their profile name didn't match their "real" name, meaning the name on state-issued ID. Facebook's insistence that people use their "real" name to open an account is a legacy of its Ivy League roots, when Facebook profiles were available only to people with a harvard.edu email address. Even after Facebook expanded to include other universities (in 2005) and eventually everyone over the age of thirteen (in 2006), the real name policy remained. The issue had produced complaints over the years, but the targeted reporting of drag queens felt trans- and homophobic. Backlash was swift and angry. When the controversy over real names came to a head, I'd been studying Brooklyn's drag community for about a year. Like many performers, drag queens spend a lot of time crafting their stage names and public personas. Some of the people I interviewed wanted to be on Facebook exclusively under their stage name; others preferred to have two profiles, to help separate the different personas and social networks that belonged to their on-stage and off-stage selves. They all felt pressured to conform to Facebook's rules, even if the rules felt overly straight and restrictive.

Drag queens weren't the only ones who cared about the issue of names—Native Americans, journalists, police informants, and survivors of sexual assault all had good reasons for wanting more flexibility around profile names. Drag queens built a coalition with these groups and launched online and offline campaigns to demand change. Eventually, Facebook gave in and changed their policy of displacing people who didn't look or sound like Facebook's ideal users. In a lot of ways, this was a victory—it's not every day that major social media companies admit a mistake and adopt new policies. But the episode left some things unresolved. Why can't people have multiple profiles? And why can't platforms give their users more agency *before* there's a major controversy?

Arguing that people should be allowed to control their online identities gets tricky when it comes to extreme or illegal content. We might want drag queens to be able to use multiple names, but not scammers or terrorists. The difference here is that drag queens (and other groups, such as Native Americans and abuse survivors) aren't using pseudonyms to commit crimes. They're actually using Facebook exactly as directed—to promote themselves and maintain relationships. We might also ask, why should platforms accommodate the needs of drag queens? Why should a company like Facebook, with two billion users, change its policies to help out a tiny percentage of people? I often get this question when I present research on how countercultural or marginalized groups are left behind by mainstream tech. My answer is that most mainstream tech companies insist that they want to be inclusive in building community. If these same companies fail, not just once, but over and over, to imagine how people on the margins might use or relate to their technology, then it's fair to ask about the depth of their commitment to inclusion.

Facebook no longer requires a direct match between a user's name and her driver's license. But the company is very much still invested in knowing exactly who its users are, as are Google, Amazon, and other Big Tech companies. The main reason for the obsession over user data has to do with advertising, which I'll unpack in the next section. But the push for real names has important links to isolation. In an article on how digital media is changing the work of music criticism, journalist Amanda Petrusich observed, "The culture of fandom is fragmented now in unprecedented ways; one is no longer required to entertain or indulge the hideous taste of others. It is possible, even encouraged, for a music fan to venture online and locate whatever niche community speaks directly to her proclivities and desires . . . and then to occupy that space, building a reinforced cottage there, among her people."

Whether it's pop music or politics, online personalization pushes us toward monotony. The internet was supposed to be the world's best bet for DIY education and self-discovery. Sometimes, it still is, whether we're talking about Wikipedia info or music on Soundcloud. But we have to be on guard when platforms push us into silos and close off access to the unexpected.

Digital Redlining and the Tyranny of Ad Revenue

Platforms with wildly different aesthetics, user bases, and norms often share one key thing: advertising. More specifically, they rely on advertising to support a profitable business model. Of course, every company wants to make money, but selling ads wasn't always the default model for making money for a social media company. Platforms (like BME, as well as Wikipedia and Craigslist) have experimented with donations and membership fees over the years. Some rely heavily on volunteer labor for moderation or technical know-how. But most websites use advertising to keep the lights on. Usually, this means that people sign up to use a platform or service for "free." Instead of paying a membership fee, users agree to have information about what they do on the site sold to advertisers. Basically, users are trading personal data for personalized content and social connectivity.

It's easier for platforms to monetize user data when they know exactly who's online. That's why most platforms want users to be as transparent as possible, while they hide as much as they can about their algorithms and advertising models. Armed with incredibly detailed data about our likes, dislikes, and social networks, advertisers can target their ads to hyperspecific groups of people. Are you a toy company looking to reach new parents aged twenty-eight to thirty-four? Are you a health food store interested in targeting vegetarians who do yoga? There are hundreds of categories for interests and identity markers that advertisers can home in on. As a result of this exchange, companies have more information about us than we have about ourselves. In an era when 66 percent of U.S. adults get their news from Facebook and more shopping happens online than IRL, digital advertising is a crucial battleground of attention, access, and literacy.

The obsession with user data and advertising produces real inequalities across the internet. Earlier, I described redlining as a practice of excluding marginalized groups from housing opportunities. On mainstream social media platforms, digital redlining takes advantage of the massive amount of user data to push products and services in a way that isn't just targeted, it's biased. At the heart of digital redlining are data brokers. Data brokers are the companies that buy and sell user data, the middlemen between social media companies and advertisers. Some people don't mind data gathering and targeted ads, while others find them creepy and intrusive. But what's at stake here is the question of how this data can be used unfairly. Through digital redlining, data brokers can target ads to groups of people based on their identities or where they live, setting up major imbalances of power. A group of activists and academics called Our Data Bodies, including Tamika Lewis, Seeta Peña Gangadharan, Mariella Saba, and Tawana Petty, came together to write the *Digital Defense Playbook,* a workbook of activities and resources to promote "data justice and data access for equity." The playbook describes a number of problems tied to the mainstream internet, particularly around how much control ordinary people have over their data: "When our data are manipulated, distorted, stolen, exploited, or misused, our communities are stifled, obstructed, or repressed and our ability to self-determine and prosper is systematically controlled." (For more on this topic, see the work of Andre Brock, Virginia Eubanks, and Safiya Noble, who have all written powerfully on the ways that Big Tech and government programs discriminate against people of color and the poor.)

Digital redlining has direct links to urban gentrification. In 2019, the Department of Housing and Urban Development (HUD) sued Facebook over housing discrimination. According to HUD,

Facebook lets advertisers push ads to users based on their "ethnic affinities" and gender, in violation of the Fair Housing Act. The 2019 HUD complaint isn't the first time Facebook has been accused of digital redlining. In 2016, ProPublica found that Facebook let advertisers hide or display ads to users based on different characteristics, including race. As a result, ads for houses or jobs could be deliberately hidden from people of color. Facebook's advertising tools barred people from certain geographic areas from seeing certain ads. The tools actually created red lines on a map to target users, a direct parallel to "redlining" practices that created housing segregation in the United States in the mid-twentieth century.

In gentrifying neighborhoods, it isn't necessarily a bad thing when new businesses open up. But new businesses become a problem when they cater to newcomers at the expense of old timers. A similar dynamic emerges when companies rely on advertising. The problem with advertising isn't really that it's commercial per se. It's how commercial profits drive an obsession over user data, which can be more costly for people on the margins. In a 2019 editorial for *Wired,* Zeynep Tufekci argued that advertising works only for the largest of internet companies because making a profit from advertising requires a massive user base. Smaller platforms will struggle as long as the advertising business model remains the best way to attract major investors. Tufekci's other key critique of advertising is tied to the attention economy. Relying on advertising requires "content creators [to] chase eyeballs and fractions of ad dollars on these giant platforms, whose business model favors virality, misinformation and outrage." Tufekci argues that the dependence on advertising leaves us all worse off. Reduced privacy, fake news, extreme content—they're all byproducts of the push for advertising dollars and the power of data brokers.

If online culture is becoming so unfair, why don't more people leave? It's difficult to leave a social media platform for a lot of the same reasons it's difficult to leave a neighborhood: it's where your friends and family are, and you've probably spent a lot of time getting settled and building local ties. Even if a neighborhood changes in ways we don't like, it can be hard to pack up our things and go. Basically, the problem with refusal is that it comes with a cost. Not everyone can opt out of social media when there's significant social or work pressure to get and stay online.

There are things users can do to push back on intrusive and biased data gathering. In their book *Obfuscation*, Finn Brunton and Helen Nissenbaum lay out a number of strategies for building literacy about online tracking and hiding—or obfuscating—personal information. They suggest installing browser plugins that track and block cookies, getting multiple people to use the same social media accounts, switching SIM cards between devices, and creating a flurry of online activity to cover your tracks. Learning more about how data is collected is crucial because we need to balance the scale between how much tech companies know about us versus how much we know about them. Even taking small steps to change our daily habits online can introduce interference into the circuit of data brokers, advertisers, and social media platforms.

Digital culture has always been in flux. Technology changes, new platforms arrive, and old ones die out. Change itself isn't the problem, it's that digital culture is evolving to support the interests of a few, with a cost for the many. In cities, gentrification reflects a tipping of the scales toward developers and newcomers, and away from longtime residents and their culture. Digital redlining shows us a direct parallel between the harms of biased data gathering and an unequal real estate market. More broadly, the big social media platforms are getting bigger, and smaller platforms are struggling to survive. If trends in digital culture continue, we'll end up with online experiences that are less diverse, more isolated, and hypercommercialized.

3 *The Big Problems of Big Tech*

Technology doesn't emerge in a vacuum; it comes from people and corporations with specific ideas about the problems tech can solve and the people who should use it. To get answers about the internet and its politics, we have to look at the goals and values of Big Tech. As Steven Johnson, a journalist from *Wired* magazine, put it, "Whatever you may think of Big Tech, it is arguably the most influential concentration of new wealth and information networks in the history of humankind. It would be good to have an accurate read on what its politics are." Gentrification gives us a way of reading Big Tech's politics, helping us to see how the industry is reshaping major cities and how its platforms reproduce inequalities and bias.

The tech industry contributes to gentrification in three key ways: tech company headquarters taking over local neighborhoods; an isolating lack of diversity in the Big Tech workforce; and a business culture that puts profits over people. Battles over urban space are the most direct link between Big Tech and gentrification, with tech sector employees leading the charge to gentrify cities that host or have nearby corporate headquarters. A second issue has to do with who gets to work in the tech industry. Like the gentrified neighborhoods being supported by Big Tech, the tech sector itself has a serious diversity problem: people who work in Big Tech are disproportionately White, male, and young. This lack of diversity matters because homogenous workforces affect the kinds of devices and platforms that are designed and promoted. Finally, I'll show how the internet has gentrified in terms of its priorities. The internet has always allowed people to make money, but after the U.S. financial recession in 2008, culture in the tech industry shifted. An influx of banking industry experts brought new priorities, which emphasized consolidating control and stamping out competitors. The result is an industry motivated by building monopolies rather than radical creativity.

No industry can be summarized as a totality. Big Tech contains thousands of companies and has produced countless products. There's no single viewpoint or set of politics that can fully capture all of them. Within every industry, and even every company, there are always avenues for dissent. Starting in 2017, mainstream tech companies like Google and Microsoft have been rocked by internal protests, walkouts, and demands to protect workers and refuse major defense contracts. I've worked for major tech and media companies (Microsoft and Viacom), so I know firsthand that big corporations have employees who don't agree with all of their decisions. Even so, there are still norms and trends that guide the industry as a whole.

By Big Tech, I mean the mainstream tech companies that put out massively popular products and services. And when I write about the tech sector in this chapter, what I'm really talking about are the dominant values that hold sway in Silicon Valley. (Silicon Valley is a major tech industry powerhouse, but there are other epicenters across the world, like Beijing, Bengaluru, Berlin, and Tel Aviv. I don't have the space to get into the ways that Silicon Valley ideology does and doesn't transfer globally, but common elements linking them together include a belief that technological progress drives social improvement, support for capitalism, and resistance to regulation.)

The belief system of Big Tech often gets called cyber-libertarianism, or the California Ideology. What goes into this value system? Big Tech tends to believe that technology is the answer to social problems. The idea that technology drives social change is called techno-determinism, meaning technology determines social outcomes. A good example of techno-determinism is the One Laptop Per Child project, which assumed that getting computers into the hands of kids in Latin America could overcome major hurdles of poverty, racism, and bias. As tech industry researcher Morgan Ames found in her years-long study of One Laptop Per Child, computers alone can't "solve" education in Latin America—or anywhere else. What's really needed is higher pay and more training for teachers, and a bigger social safety net.

Another key feature of Big Tech's value system is meritocracy. In theory, meritocracy is a good thing because it emphasizes the ability to do something and (supposedly) ignores identity markers like race and gender. The problem is, getting encouragement and resources for training in tech is often tied to race, class, and gender. In practice, meritocracy often fails to take into account the ways that the odds are stacked against certain groups.

The last feature of cyber libertarians to keep in mind is that they tend to be socially liberal but prefer a hands-off approach when it comes to federal regulation. People who believe in the California Ideology usually don't mind paying their taxes (or creating nonprofits to tackle social problems), but they don't want the government to oversee the tech sector. Together, these values speak to a worldview that advocates for social change, but with technological solutions and no meaningful challenge to capitalism. (For more on Silicon Valley's politics and values, check out work by Megan Sapnar Ankerson and Fred Turner.)

When Big Tech Is Your Neighbor

For most of this book, I use gentrification as a metaphor for thinking about the politics of digital technologies. But there are also some very literal connections between urban gentrification and Big Tech, like what happens to a city or neighborhood when tech companies move in and set up shop. Many cities work feverishly to bring Big Tech within city limits, believing that these companies will boost employment and local business. In 2018, Amazon announced its plans to open a second corporate headquarters (the first is in Seattle). The news set off a frenzy among cities across the United States. Local governments bent over backward to offer tax breaks and other incentives, like promises to increase public transit and add green space. Amazon finally announced plans to open two new headquarters, one just outside of Washington, D.C., and one in the New York City borough of Queens. The plans for a Queens headquarters fell apart after resistance from local activists and lawmakers, and a key talking point for activists revolved around a question: Why would local governments offer tax breaks to one of the richest companies in the world?

After years of not turning a profit, Amazon is now one of the most profitable companies in the world. The company reported record profits in 2018, earning $10.1 billion in net income, as documented by Andrew Davis at CNBC. That same year, Amazon paid $0 in U.S. federal income tax. In fact, Amazon received a

$129 million tax rebate from the federal government. While workers in Amazon warehouses are on the hook for paying income tax, the company itself actually gets paid to exist. And local governments have been happy to follow the federal example, offering tax breaks to this fantastically rich company while ignoring calls for affordable housing. Urban studies researcher Richard Florida described Amazon's search for a second headquarters as a "catastrophic" setback for improving economic development. He argued that incentives "set up fake competitions to game the process and extract incentives. Politicians play the game to the hilt, even when they know it's bad policy, because they think vying for the trophy makes them look good and wins votes."

It doesn't take Amazon-level profits to get red carpet treatment from local governments. Tech companies often take advantage of the assumption that it's smart (and profitable) for a town or neighborhood to have a major corporation to set up shop there. But it turns out that luring corporate offices into town isn't always such a good deal. According to economist Amihai Glazer, offering tax incentives to major corporations tends to backfire for a few key reasons. First, there's no punishment if corporations fail to live up to their end of the deal, meaning that they get tax breaks even if down the road there are layoffs or the company folds. Second, companies almost never generate more income for a city than what gets spent on incentives. It also turns out that most of the time (75 percent!), tax incentives don't play a major role in a company's decision making, meaning that the company would have moved there even without the promise of a bargain. Finally, Glazer found that companies that take tax incentives are slightly more likely to fail than companies that don't. So statistically, no one seems to win when cities offer corporate tax breaks as an incentive to move.

But let's say you weren't as lucky as Queens in dodging Big Tech. What happens when tech companies do move in? They put pressure on the real estate market, and previously affordable neighborhoods are overwhelmed by employees moving to the area. In addition to increasing competition for housing, Big Tech can decrease demand for businesses nearby. By supplying their employees with free lunches, snacks, and even beer, tech companies actually reduce foot traffic to local restaurants. And then there are the tax loopholes I mentioned earlier. So the same companies that increase cost of living and decrease quality of life for their neighbors also evade corporate taxes that could go to public resources like schools and roads. Taking all of these drawbacks together, Big Tech is less of a boon to the local economy than it is a burden on the surrounding neighborhoods.

Some of the most intense battles over the tech industry's role in gentrification are taking place in Northern California. Although the tech industry took root in Silicon Valley in the 1940s and '50s, the problem of gentrification has gotten noticeably worse in the past twenty years. I grew up in the Bay Area in the 1990s, during the first boom of the tech industry. Local companies like Google and Apple developed technologies that made a huge difference in the lives of ordinary Californians (as elsewhere in the world), but they didn't have a huge impact on housing in nearby cities like San Francisco and Oakland. At the time, the tech industry was concentrated in Silicon Valley, aka the South Bay. Like hardware companies before them, software companies mostly stayed in the suburbs of San Jose, like Cupertino and Palo Alto.

The post-2008 recession tech boom, however, was something else entirely. Across the United States, young people were moving to cities in record numbers. In Northern California's big cities, tech companies paved the way, luring young people with signing bonuses and special perks. Companies provided chartered buses to transport employees between San Francisco and the South Bay. As a result, even though their headquarters were miles outside of city limits, tech companies still created major problems. In San Francisco and Oakland, the sudden increase in wealthier residents put pressure on real estate markets that had mostly served low-income or middle-class POC. My friends who grew up and stayed in the Bay Area often trade horror stories of how fierce the housing market has become. Properties can go for hundreds of thousands over asking price, and buyers have shown up to open houses with enough cash to purchase a home outright. The result is that Northern California's big cities are getting more unequal and less diverse. In the past twenty-five years, San Francisco, San Jose, and Oakland have seen drastic decreases in their POC populations, while the number of wealthy White residents has skyrocketed. San Francisco was initially the epicenter of the problem, but gentrification has spread to other cities nearby. In Oakland, displacement is skewed heavily toward African American households and families with children. According to a report from Policy Link, between 2000 and 2010, the Oakland Unified School District lost more than ten thousand POC students and the City of Oakland lost thirty-four thousand African American residents, representing a 24 percent decline. In a single year between 2015 and 2016, the average rent for an available two-bedroom apartment in Oakland increased by 25 percent. Big Tech isn't the only industry driving these changes, but it's become the most public face of a battle between corporate wealth and local community.

There are many, many stories of people (mostly White dudes) from the tech sector doing racist and classist things in rapidly gentrifying neighborhoods. These encounters illustrate tensions of privilege and entitlement. To give a couple examples: In 2014, some Dropbox employees—who were wearing corporate-branded T-shirts—kicked a bunch of local kids off a San Francisco soccer field. The Dropbox employees insisted that they had "reserved" the field through a smartphone app, never mind that the (mostly Latinx) kids had been playing ball on that playground their whole lives. In March 2019, a group of wealthy San Franciscans created a GoFundMe page to raise money to fight a new resource center for people experiencing homelessness. The campaign raised over $100,000 to pay for a lawyer to protest the legality of the shelter. (Using crowdfunding to fight homeless shelters has become a tactic across the country—a search on GoFundMe and other fundraising platforms turns up dozens of similar examples.) Meanwhile, a counter-protest site raised over $175,000 in support of the resource center. Later that year, the original naysayers lost their battle with the city, and the resource center got the green light to move forward. But the NIMBY attitude of the original campaign demonstrates what kind of neighbors gentrifiers can be.

The example that I find most useful for thinking about what it feels like to have tech bros as neighbors comes from a 2015 incident, also in San Francisco (and described by Michael Miller in the *Chicago Tribune*). Justin Keller, a developer and start-up founder moved to San Francisco in 2012. Three years later, he wrote an open letter to San Francisco's mayor and chief of police demanding action on the local homeless population. In the letter, Keller complained that, "Every day, on my way to, and from work, I see people sprawled across the sidewalk, tent cities, human feces, and the faces of addiction. The city is becoming a shanty town." Keller went on to acknowledge that gentrification is on a lot of people's minds, but he refused to take any responsibility for his role in the city's problems: "I know people are frustrated about gentrification happening in the city, but the reality is, we live in a free market society. The wealthy working people have earned their right to live in the city. They went out, got an education, work hard, and earned it." Keller's letter, which also referred to homeless people as "riff raff," helps us see the dangerous side of Big Tech's belief in meritocracy and capitalism. For Keller, meritocracy means that people who work hard get rewarded. But on the flip side, people who have nothing must not have worked hard. It's probably true that Keller and people like him have put in a lot of work for the successes they've had. But it doesn't follow that people who don't have a high-paying job or a fancy apartment are lazy and undeserving. For folks like Keller, gentrification is a positive force for change, part of the natural cycle behind capitalist societies. From Keller's point of view, gentrification hasn't gone far enough in San Francisco—there hasn't been enough displacement, and the city is still too diverse. People like Keller hear gentrification and think "progress," and to them, gentrification is just another word for capitalism. But as urban studies researcher Neil Smith insists, "For those impoverished, evicted or made homeless in its wake, gentrification is indeed a dirty word and it should stay a dirty word."

What's ironic about the tech industry's relationship to Bay Area gentrification is that Big Tech is displacing the same communities that inspired the radical creativity of the early internet in the United States. Media historian Fred Turner has written about the countercultural roots of digital technology, from hippy communes to Burning Man. Yet it seems that Big Tech mostly pays lip service to these countercultural values while displacing the communities at its core. As Olivia Solon, a tech journalist for the *Guardian*, observed of the Bay Area, "Here was a counterculture whose language and sensibility the tech industry sometimes adopts, but whose practitioners it has mostly priced out."

Increasingly, tech companies have realized that they're a big part of the housing crises surrounding their headquarters. The motivation for addressing these problems isn't so much altruistic as pragmatic: it's hard to recruit people for jobs in cities where housing is totally unaffordable. Buying a home in San Francisco, Oakland, or their surrounding suburbs has become out of reach, even for people making six-figure salaries. In 2019, Google announced that it would make a $1 billion investment over the next ten years to build twenty thousand units of housing. As Vivian Ho reported in the *Guardian*, $750 million of the funds will go to converting existing Google office space into fifteen thousand housing units. Google also donated $50 million to nonprofits that tackle homelessness. The rest of the money was set aside as "incentives" for developers to build five thousand units of affordable housing. It's great that Google recognizes its role in gentrification and is willing to throw money at the problem. But there are still some major unknowns about Google's plans to fight gentrification. It's unclear how much of the new housing will go to Google employees versus other folks, and the ratio of affordable housing to high-cost housing still isn't in line with what local activists have been calling for. Above all, we have to remember—Google is essentially trying to solve a problem that it helped create.

Other companies have gone the route of Zapier, a San Francisco–based startup that automates different web apps to work together. In 2017, the company started a new "de-location" program that offers its employees $10,000 to move out of the Bay

Area. This initiative takes advantage of digital communication and disrupts the idea that tech employees have to live in Silicon Valley. Responding to COVID-19 in 2020, many tech companies asked their employees (the ones who weren't laid off) to work from home. Companies like Twitter and Square announced that these changes would be permanent, which could have long-term consequences for Silicon Valley as the nexus of Big Tech. None of these changes mean much to low-paid workers and support staff, who usually don't have access to these benefits (and are usually laid off or furloughed instead). The tech industry sees itself as forward thinking and solutions focused, so we should demand creative solutions to problems that they're creating or exacerbating. But gentrification is too big of an issue to solve solely by relying on piecemeal experiments and altruism from individual companies. We also need local housing regulation and widespread social pressure around industry norms.

What would being a better neighbor look like? Tech companies often have people called "community managers," and it's their job to encourage collaboration and engagement in the workforce. What if the job description was reoriented toward collaboration and engagement with the local community? Rather than trying to boost morale and collaboration among coworkers, community managers could work as a bridge to local communities by developing relationships and addressing problems. Instead of spending ludicrous amounts of money on extravagant holiday parties and swag, what if tech companies put more resources into local schools, infrastructure, and housing initiatives? Tech companies also need to stop asking for tax breaks—and local governments should stop offering them. There's not a lot of data that says tax breaks are good for the companies that take them, and there's overwhelming evidence that they're bad for the cities that offer them. Being a better neighbor should be a top-down and bottom-up effort, where companies are as creative in coming up with housing solutions as they are in developing new products, and employees are as committed to their neighborhoods as they are to innovative technology.

Maybe the best ideas for how Big Tech can be a better neighbor come from people who have seen firsthand what kinds of changes happen when major tech companies move in. In 2019, Yolanda Chavez wrote an open letter to Google's CEO, Sundar Pichai. As an immigrant and activist who raised a family in San Jose, California, Chavez had major concerns about Google's plans to open up a new campus in her adopted home. She also had some solid, practical advice on how tech companies can be better neighbors:

> Your new mega-campus will rely on thousands of service workers to cook, clean, protect, and drive Google buses. These people are far more likely to be Latino and African American than the rest of your workforce. Will you ensure they have a voice on the job and the freedom to join together to negotiate better working conditions? Will you take steps to hire future engineers and programmers from San José and help provide more children in our community with education and training opportunities to prepare for these jobs?

Chavez's letter is an important reminder that gentrification isn't just a metaphor for the relationships between people and Big Tech. In some cases, the relationship between community ties, affordable housing and tech industry politics is very literal, the stakes are very high, and the need for local action is immediate.

Life in a Filter Bubble: Big Tech's Diversity Problem

The tech industry shares another feature with gentrified neighborhoods: isolation. In 2018, a blog post by Mark Luckie, a Facebook employee, went viral. Luckie worked as a strategic partner manager for global influencers, but he quit shortly after writing the post, which called out Facebook for ignoring Black users and alienating Black employees. He argued that microaggressions against POC were rampant at Facebook, that appeals to human resources were usually a dead end, and that efforts at inclusion were halfhearted. The post provided an insider's look at one of the internet's most important companies, and the view turned out to be grim. In explaining why he planned to leave Facebook, Luckie wrote, "To continue to witness and be in the center of the systematic disenfranchisement of underrepresented voices, however unintentional, is more than I'm willing to sacrifice personally." Luckie is just one of many Big Tech employees who've pulled back the curtain on their companies, exposing their blinders, biases, and failures. One thread that cuts across this genre of Big Tech tell-alls is the need to include different viewpoints and perspectives. Without more diversity inside Big Tech, its products and users will continue to be "in the center of systematic disenfranchisement."

While Luckie was calling out Facebook for its superficial commitment to inclusion, Google was quietly cutting its diversity initiatives. Starting in 2018, internal diversity and inclusion programs at the company have been scaled back or axed entirely. In 2019, employees who worked full-time on diversity training were reassigned to other projects. (In response, ten Democrats in Congress asked Google to explain reports about its waning commitment to diversity.) Training isn't the only (or even the best) way to support social justice in the tech industry, but it's an important signal of a company's politics and priorities. So what does it mean when a company as powerful as Google pulls the plug on programming that supports social justice and equality?

For people who study technology and ethics, calling out the lack of diversity in the tech industry is a pretty worn argument. But just because we've heard the complaint before doesn't mean the problem has been resolved. In fact, the lack of diversity in the tech workforce has been an incredibly stubborn problem. Compared to overall private industry, the U.S. tech industry employs a larger share of White people (68.5 percent in the tech industry versus 63.5 percent in the private sector) and men (64 percent in tech versus 52 percent in the private sector). When women are employed in Big Tech, it's often in "soft skill" positions like human resources or user experience rather than in coding or development. The tech industry also employs a smaller share of Black (7.4 percent in tech versus 14.4 percent in the private sector) and Latinx (8 percent in tech versus 13.9 percent in the private sector) workers, according to a 2016 report from the U.S. Equal Employment Opportunity Commission. The same report reveals that racial and gender biases get worse at the leadership levels—when it looked at tech executives, it found that 83 percent were White and 80 percent were men.

Another form of discrimination in Big Tech revolves around age. According to Alex Hern, a journalist writing for the *Guardian*, the average age of a Facebook employee is twenty-nine—at Amazon, it's thirty. In 2019, Google settled a lawsuit alleging age discrimination. The company wouldn't admit wrongdoing but agreed to pay out $11 million to more than two hundred applicants who were all over forty when they first applied for jobs at Google. With stats and reports about this level of ageism, we have to ask:

How are tech companies going to take the needs of middle-aged and older people seriously when they won't even hire them as employees?

Homogenous workplaces make homogenous products. As data scientists Catherine D'Ignazio and Lauren Klein have argued, "Who any particular system is designed for, and who that system is designed by, are both issues that matter deeply. They matter because the biases they encode, and often unintentionally amplify, remain unseen and unaddressed. . . . Without women and people of color more involved in the coding and design process, the new research questions that might yield groundbreaking results don't even get asked—because they're not around to ask them." In other words, the tech industry's lack of diversity produces filter bubbles. Full of people of the same age, isolated from racial and gender diversity, the tech industry produces devices and platforms that make sense for them and often fails to see how those products leave others behind. Facial recognition software that doesn't recognize POC, voice recognition that can't handle accents, handheld devices that literally don't fit in women's hands—there are a number of embarrassing examples of tech industry blind spots caused by filter bubbles.

Segregated, isolated platforms lead to bias and discrimination. In response, new platforms are being designed to deal with bias. For example, Innclusive was created as a reaction to discrimination on the room renting company Airbnb. Studies found that POC were less likely to be selected as hosts and guests by White users. Innclusive deals with the problem by hiding the names and photos of users until both parties agree to a rental. Similarly, there's Blendoor, which launched in 2014. Writing in the *New Yorker*, Anna Weiner described Blendoor as "a hybrid of LinkedIn and Tinder, but with a twist: résumés, scrubbed of personally identifying details (photos, names, and graduation years, which can inspire racial, gender, and age bias) are presented to employers, who swipe right when they like the credentials they see." The tricky thing about these platforms is that they rely on technological solutions to fix human problems. The answer to biased humans? Build rational, reliable, unbiased platforms! But the fact is, *people* are biased—and since people write code, algorithms are biased too. We can't code our way out of this problem, at least not until we build up more digital literacy, more tools for confronting structures of digital power, and a more diverse workforce in Big Tech.

When tech companies do recruit more diverse workforces, they're sometimes accused of reverse discrimination. In 2018, tech journalist Aaron Aupperlee described how the language learning app Duolingo managed to hire an all-women cohort of software engineers. When Duolingo proudly announced these details on Facebook, a number of commenters accused the company of lowering its standards—because, they argued, obviously the only way to increase the number of women was to decrease the skills requirements for programmers. Duolingo's CEO, Luis von Ahn, responded publicly on Facebook, saying, "I am disappointed that the top comments to our post were all from men angrily arguing discrimination, and that we should hire the best people instead of worrying about hiring women. To these dudes, I say: go back to the 1970s and stay there. Idiots." It turns out that it's not actually that hard to hire more women in tech: Duolingo focused their recruitment efforts on universities with a high concentration of women in their computer science programs. (Those universities included Massachusetts Institute of Technology, Duke, Cornell, Harvard, Stanford, and Carnegie Mellon.) Another strategy involved seeking out women's groups at universities and sponsoring the 2017 Grace Hopper Conference, which is the world's largest annual meet-up for women in tech. Duolingo made a point of sending all its women engineers to the conference, where they met with hundreds of potential recruits. These efforts take time and resources, but they show that creating a more diverse workforce is doable.

Even if people don't buy the ethical or design reasons for making sure that a company's workforce is diverse, disparities come with real financial costs. For underrepresented minorities in Big Tech, the workplace can feel unwelcoming or even hostile. It's easy to feel unwelcome or isolated when no one else in your department or organization looks like you. As Mark Luckie, the former Facebook employee, wrote of his experiences at the company, "To feel like an oddity at your own place of employment because of the color of your skin while passing posters reminding you to be your authentic self feels in itself inauthentic." Luckie's experiences of isolation and aggression were representative of a bigger problem. According to a 2017 study from the Kapor Center for Social Impact, feeling marginalized at work leads people to quit in numbers that should make employers take diversity seriously. Unfairness or mistreatment within a work environment was cited as the number one reason for leaving a tech job. It was named more often than looking for a better opportunity, dissatisfaction with the work environment, being recruited away, or dissatisfaction with job responsibilities. Even aside from the push for inclusion, companies generally want their employees to stick around because hiring and training new workers takes time and resources. Pushing back on workplace filter bubbles can produce more equitable and exciting tech, and it can also boost morale and improve retention rates.

Gentrification happens when there's a major transformation in a local population. So it's fair to ask if the metaphor of gentrification still holds if the tech industry was always homogenous. Big Tech has always been mostly White and male, but there was a time when the United States did a much better job with at least getting women into STEM fields (if not so much with POC). The number of women studying computer science in the United States peaked at 37 percent in 1984, largely because of Cold War competition with the Soviet Union. Between the space race and the threat of nuclear war, the U.S. Department of Education made a push to get more women into STEM, with efforts that started in elementary school. In 2014, thirty years later, the number of women graduating with computer science degrees dropped almost by half, to 18 percent. It's sobering to think that the threat of nuclear war is what it takes to get schools, businesses, and social norms to get behind the idea of women in STEM.

While the United States isn't alone in having a homogenous tech sector, there are countries that do a much better job of bringing women into the industry. According to a 2017 report by ShowTech, Russia has more women in tech than anywhere else in the world. Women tech workers in Russia point to widespread social norms (like encouragement from parents) and having women role models in STEM fields as key factors that bring women into tech. Australia is another leader for women in tech, with women in 31 percent of IT roles. In Malaysia, the Universiti Teknologi Petronas has an impressive 61 percent enrollment of women in its computer science program, while Chang Gung University in Taiwan and Mahidol University in Thailand come close to a 50/50 breakdown of women and men in their computer science courses. At the university level, hiring women faculty in

STEM fields, organizing all-women lab support groups, and establishing peer mentoring programs can make a difference. It's important to keep these international success stories in mind so that we can challenge stubborn ideas about "natural ability" or "inclination" for tech, and as a reminder that diversity is achievable.

Getting more qualified women and people of color into the tech industry would be a major step toward equality, but what happens when they get jobs and find an unwelcoming workplace? The tech industry often emphasizes meritocracy, meaning that people are supposed to succeed based solely on their abilities. But a belief in meritocracy falls flat in the midst of overwhelming evidence of sexual harassment and discrimination. Amazon, Microsoft, Google, and Tesla have all battled accusations of gender pay gaps and inappropriate work environments. The question of workforce diversity isn't just about fairness in hiring. Big Tech's diversity problem matters in terms of design values and filter bubbles. To build better tech, we have to ask, Who's in the room when major policies get made, who gets to speak back to people in power, and who gets to see themselves in the technology they use?

Vilifying Big Tech is not the answer to the issue of its isolated workforce of filter bubbles. I don't think Big Tech has a diversity problem because people in management are set on being racist, sexist, ageist, ableist, or classist. Most of them probably see the value of a diverse workplace, for reasons that are financial as well as ethical. And yet a lack of diversity continues to be a big problem for Big Tech. We should resist a gentrified tech workforce for the same reason that people resist gentrifying neighborhoods: isolated populations create unwelcoming and unequal environments. And in Big Tech, that means tools and platforms get created that are biased, unethical, or just downright boring.

Profits over People—and the Dangers of the IPO Fairytale

So far, I've argued that the tech industry's gentrification problems revolve around inequality and diversity. As neighbors, Big Tech companies contribute to massive wealth gaps among people living in the same neighborhood. As employers, they have repeatedly failed to build more diverse workforces. The last feature of gentrification that I'll walk us through has to do with Big Tech monopolies and profit schemes. The problem with new businesses in gentrified neighborhoods isn't that they make money, it's how and for whom. The tech industry is facing a similar battle over its corporate strategies. Since 2008, the business model of Big Tech has shifted, with real impacts for ordinary users at the end of the networked line. Big Tech has become promonopoly and anticompetition, which jacks up costs to users and squashes innovation.

For believers in the California Ideology, tech can and should solve big social problems. But the real reason for the industry is to make money—lots of money. The internet has always attracted business and investment. But over time, the emphasis has shifted from technological creativity to focusing on profits and building monopolies. How did this happen? Why did the tech industry's priorities change? According to tech journalists and industry insiders, the 2008 recession eliminated Wall Street as the go-to industry for new job recruits in the United States. Looking to seek their fortunes somewhere else, a surge of elite business talent moved to Silicon Valley. In 2008, 20 percent of business school graduates worked in finance and 12 percent worked in tech, according to Nathaniel Meyersohn, a journalist for CNN. A decade later, those percentages have switched, with 13 percent of MBAs working in finance and 17 percent working in tech.

Getting into the norms and values of business schools would take another book, but industry experts say that the infusion of finance culture has changed Big Tech's priorities. Tech journalist Olivia Solon interviewed dozens of tech workers about how the industry climate changed after 2008. One of her interviewees put it this way: "The focus of Silicon Valley used to be innovation with the wonderful bonus of money on the side of that, but those two things seem to have switched." Ellen Pao has spent her career in Big Tech, including a stint as CEO of Reddit. In an interview with Noah Kulwin for *New York Magazine,* Pao described what she saw as the major shift in tech industry culture: "In 2008, when the markets crashed, all those people who are motivated by money ended up coming out to Silicon Valley. . . . And that's when values shifted more. There was, like, an optimism early around good coming out of the internet that ended up getting completely distorted in the 2000s, when you had these people coming in with a different idea and a different set of goals."

How has business school culture changed the tech industry? For one thing, the dominant business model of Big Tech has become anticompetitive in the extreme. In the early days of the tech industry, startups hustled in a collective rivalry for funding, talent, and innovation. This led to a bubble of value and hype, but it also led to new technology. Now the industry is more stable but less open. When a new product or platform starts competing with Facebook, Facebook simply buys out the upstart company and adds it to its portfolio. Facebook on its own is huge, but with Instagram and WhatsApp, it's a staggering monopoly. Microsoft and Google have grown similarly massive in the same way, by scooping up and merging with upstart competitors. In the most recent ethos of Big Tech, the goal isn't about competing to make the best tech, it's to consolidate control and eliminate competitors.

Criticizing the profiteering of Big Tech might make me sound like a radical Marxist. But by being -anticompetitive, tech companies are actually being anticapitalist. The whole idea of a free market economy is that companies compete with each other for customers, which is supposed to spur innovation and keep prices low for consumers. Monopolies clamp down on open markets, restricting the flow of ideas and capital. This is why we have antitrust laws, or rules put in place to keep companies or an industry from getting too powerful. The movement toward anticompetition is good only for early investors and is a real burden on everyone else.

There are both political and economic arguments against monopolies. Lina Khan made headlines in tech and business sections of newspapers after she published a 2016 article about Amazon in the *Yale Law Review*. Khan's main point was that we should go back to how we thought of antitrust law in the early twentieth century. For a long time in the United States, antitrust was based on protecting consumer choice. The idea was that regulation made sure that markets offered choices. Things started to change in the 1980s, when antitrust law became narrower. In this new view, antitrust law could be used only if monopolies raised their prices. This new definition of antitrust led to a wave of corporate mergers. In 1985, there were around 2,300 corporate mergers in the United States, according to statistics published by M. Szmigiera on Statista. In 2017, just under thirty years later, there were more than 15,300. The updated definition of antitrust is hard to apply to Big Tech because many of the biggest players in the Tech Industry don't actually charge users for their services. Facebook and Google are the same cost to use—$0. Khan argued that an older reading of antitrust law would regulate predatory pricing and vertical integration, two crucial factors in Amazon's business model. Although she hadn't yet passed the bar, Khan's article went viral, at least by the standards of dense legal writing. While many tech critics had argued that Big Tech needed to be regulated, Khan offered a specific framework for limiting their growth.

Khan isn't the only one turning to antitrust laws to regulate Big Tech. Senator and 2020 presidential hopeful Elizabeth Warren called out companies like Facebook for being too big. During her campaign, she promised to make reforming Big Tech part of her economic policy. Another voice calling for antitrust reform is law professor Tim Wu. Wu believes that monopolies are antidemocratic and argues that we need antitrust regulations to protect small businesses and consumer choice. If new businesses are going to have any chance of success, there has to be a level playing field. Startups need time to experiment and grow as they develop new products and establish a business plan. Monopolies skew market forces and limit innovation from newcomers. According to economist Jonathan Baker, we need antitrust laws to protect markets. Baker argues that Big Tech is responsible for creating "wonders of the modern world," but he also asks "whether some aspects of their conduct limit competition, thereby preventing consumers, workers, and the economy as a whole from benefiting even more." We don't really have to choose between politics and economics, they're just different ways of focusing on the same problem: monopolies create unhealthy, homogenous marketplaces.

Urban gentrification is also tied to monopolies, as I mentioned in the first chapter. In many neighborhoods, gentrification is driven by a small number of powerful developers. Able to operate at scale, raise massive amounts of cash, and negotiate directly with local policymakers, these developers hoard resources and exclude smaller, local players from entering the market. Monopolies in Big Tech are similarly dangerous if we want open, democratic markets, not to mention innovative, inclusive technology.

We could ask, If people like the platform, why is it a problem if Facebook is a monopoly? In some places, Facebook has essentially monopolized access to the internet, so much so that people don't realize that being on Facebook means being online. When a think tank surveyed Indonesians in 2012, many of the respondents spoke enthusiastically about using Facebook but said that they did not use the internet. As tech journalist Sophie Curtis explained, "If large numbers of first-time adopters come online via Facebook's proprietary network, rather than via the open web, their whole understanding the internet will be distorted." At the same time, policymakers, businesses, community organizations, and media publishers will feel pressured to use Facebook as their main communication platform if they want to reach customers and constituents. When Facebook monopolizes someone's entire experience of being online, their control isn't just technological, it's social, cultural, and political.

Does it have to be this way? Are there other workable business models for Big Tech? It's very possible that this next argument will get the most pushback from otherwise on-board readers, because I'm going to argue that for gentrification to stop taking over the internet, companies are going to have to change their relationships to profits—and in some cases, maybe make less money. When you live in a capitalist society, the idea of asking companies to make less money feels absurd, like you might as well suggest dragons as a form of transportation. But the tech industry's relationship to profits and competition can and must be challenged.

The tech field has seen some very profitable companies that have simply opted to make less money in order to live up to a set of values. Take Craigslist, for example. The media company AIM estimated that Craigslist brought in $1.034 billion in 2018, an increase of nearly 50 percent from its 2016 revenue. Craigslist makes money in a very straightforward way—it charges a small fee to post certain kinds of ads, mostly real estate listings and job ads. (This is a much more transparent business model than what happens with most online platforms, where advertising models are hidden and users are often unclear on how profits are being made.) The company makes a lot of money, but it could make even more by hosting banner ads or monetizing user behavior. Yet for more than two decades, Craigslist has refused to maximize profits because they're ethically opposed to banner ads and monetizing user behavior.

Founder Craig Newmark has summed up his priorities for the company with the phrase "Doing well by doing good." In a company blog post, Craigslist's CEO Jim Buckmaster spelled out his reasoning for the "profit minimalism" approach that guides the company's leadership: "Craig Newmark and I have been called communists and socialists for putting community ahead of financial considerations. . . . To the eternal amazement of financial analysts we have never sought to maximize our personal gain. Not because we're saints, but because valuing service over money is more fulfilling and enjoyable, and has always felt like the right thing to do."

For Newmark and Buckmaster, the ideal business model is one that aligns with their values rather than one that maximizes profits. I'm not saying that Craigslist is a perfect company or that its business model would work for every tech company. But Craigslist is an important example of a longstanding, highly successful platform that has resisted the business models and narratives of Big Tech. Craigslist's longevity and success show that it's possible to turn a profit without sacrificing user data and privacy.

There's a crucial reason that Craigslist can refuse to post banner ads and opt out of maximizing profits—the company is privately held. Craigslist has never had more than three shareholders, and currently all shares are held by Buckmaster and Newmark. People often think of private companies as less transparent, which is true. Shareholder reports reveal a lot about a company's investments, profits, and internal structure. But there's a tradeoff. Once shareholders are involved, companies have what's called fiduciary responsibility—an obligation to maximize profits and increase the value of shares. Taking a company public is a step down a path that can't be undone, and it has crucial consequences for end users.

What we need is a new narrative of what makes a tech company "successful." Since the 1990s, a powerful story about tech industry success has become dominant. In this story, a couple of guys (and as I noted earlier, it's almost always men) have a zany idea for a product. They build and fail, fail and build until finally they launch a product that picks up a massive, even cult-like following. Finally, they take their company public, meaning that individual investors from the public can buy shares in the company. This is the Cinderella moment when early investors and employees who were offered company stock as a form of payment reap the rewards by selling shares to the public. Jeff Bezos and Amazon, Travis Kalanick and Uber, Mark Zuckerberg and Facebook, Elon Musk and Tesla—they all followed the same fairy tale script of the IPO payout. Big Tech's IPO model is meant to reward early investors and employees who got in on the ground floor. But the IPO is also a key moment of loss, because from that point forward, companies have to put shareholders ahead of users. Believing in the IPO narrative as the definition of a tech company's success fundamentally limits the ability to privilege users over the financial bottom line.

We need new narratives for success in Big Tech, and maybe even new definitions of what makes a company a tech company. Why is Airbnb a tech company but Hilton a hotel company? Both exist to match people with vacation spots. Why is Uber a tech company but Avis a rental car company? Both use websites and apps to get people driving. When we label Airbnb, Amazon, and Uber as tech companies, it gives them a pass when it comes to regulation. Uber and Lyft have fought hard to label themselves as companies that match users with services rather than as car companies specifically because they want to avoid regulation around how they treat their employees. In a conversation I had with tech activist Alison Macrina in May 2020, she asked, "What would happen if we started thinking of tech companies as antiregulation companies?" In addition to implementing antitrust laws, union organizing, environmental protections, and (as we'll see in the next chapter) net neutrality could all be more doable if we changed our labels, and our expectations, for Big Tech.

The call for Big Tech to experiment with different business models isn't radical or even anticapitalist. It has a parallel with antigentrification activists who aren't opposed to private businesses in their neighborhoods, just to the kinds of profiteering businesses that tend to show up. Developers might be able to make the most money by selling commercial properties to the highest bidders, but they could also turn a profit by prioritizing locally and POC-owned businesses. We should make similar demands of tech companies, by calling for business models that don't exploit users for the sake of maximizing profits and building monopolies.

What would new narratives for success in Big Tech sound like? Alternatives of successful tech could emphasize their inclusivity or sustainability. We demand diversity from Hollywood and green alternatives from car manufacturers. While these campaigns have a long way to go, we need at least this much agitation around diversity and sustainability in Big Tech. If this sounds too upbeat or naive, it's not because alternative narratives are untenable but because Big Tech has persuaded us that there's no other way. A gentrified tech industry leaves us all worse off. Big Tech has spurred on urban gentrification, with neighborhoods getting pricier and losing their longtime residents. An isolated, segregated workforce leads to problematic products. There's plenty of money in the tech industry without building monopolies at the expense of ordinary internet users.

4 *The Fight for Fiber*

Over time, computers have become easier to use and the internet easier to access. It used to be that people needed special training to be able to use software on a machine. Now, small children can do it. Instead of connecting through the long, noisy process of dial-up, our devices can now connect to the internet (and each other) instantly, without human intervention or even awareness. Mostly, this is a good thing. More intuitive design means more people are getting online and more have access to powerful tools for self-expression and community. It would be excruciating to try to use sophisticated online tools and platforms with old-school modems and routers. One advantage, though, of older technologies is that they forced us to think about what was under the hood of the devices we used every day. The clicking, whirring, and beeping of old-school dial-up modems made it obvious that digital connections don't just magically appear—they have to be built and maintained. The problem with seamless technology is that it's easier for tech companies to control users when the underlying operations are hidden and mysterious. Demanding change starts with understanding how technology works, who owns it, and how it's regulated.

It's easy to ignore the physical components that make up the internet—after all, the cables and fiber responsible for online connectivity are literally out of sight, buried underground and stretched under the sea. Terms like *cloud computing* and *wireless connection* make it seem like technology is effortless and abstract, operating in the ether. But as researchers like Tung-Hui Hu and Nicole Starosielski have argued, there are *always* literal, concrete materials involved in our digital technologies. When we pull back the curtain on the internet's infrastructure, we expose different technical layers, like cables and wires, towers and satellites. In addition to these technical features, digital infrastructure includes the legal frameworks and rules that govern online life. From the very first packet switches of the internet, policy debates have shaped who gets to go online and how much access costs. Urban gentrification doesn't happen spontaneously, it requires local policymakers to side with developers over longtime residents. The online parallel I trace in this chapter revolves around cooperation between major communication companies and government regulators. Commercialization and inequality are key features of gentrification, and they also describe a transformation in who controls access to the internet.

In the United States, the infrastructure of the internet is controlled by a monopoly of companies called internet service providers (ISPs). As the gatekeepers of the fiber and cable that keeps the internet alive, ISPs decide how much power and choice users have online. How much does your monthly internet cost? How fast is it? Did it come bundled with a phone and cable TV package? Are you on a monthly contract? And maybe most important, if you wanted to switch to another provider, could you? The answers to these questions aren't really determined by anything technical—they're determined by the business interests and regulation of ISPs. Before people open a browser or log into an app, their ability to access the internet is shaped and manipulated by ISPs, which is why we have to look at the history and politics of these companies.

In 2016, the United Nations declared internet access to be a basic human right, as fundamental as food, water, and freedom of movement. So you might think that governments would take the task of making sure people can get online seriously. Yet U.S. companies controlling the cost and speed of internet access have almost entirely escaped government regulation, meaning that they have been allowed to pursue profits rather than prioritize access to technologies that are increasingly central for everyday work and social life. It wasn't always this way. In its early days, the U.S. internet was tightly controlled by government agencies like the National Science Foundation (NSF). This period of federal oversight was followed by a wave of ISP startups, which were often scrappy, ragtag, and hyperlocal. The messy diversity of early ISPs was followed by a consolidation of power, driven by commercial interests rather than consumer demand. Without meaningful regulation, ISPs are free to pursue profits and ignore the needs of consumers. The lack of competition in the ISP market is bad for everyone, but it's an extra burden on people who are poor and geographically isolated.

This chapter digs into the history of ISPs, and I'll argue that they've gentrified, with smaller, community-based ISPs getting pushed out by national conglomerates. The result is a more homogenous and much more commercial landscape. This leaves the average internet user worse off, with fewer choices and less freedom. Remembering a moment in the history of the internet when providers were more local and community focused can help us push back on the gentrified system we have now.

Key Terms in Digital Infrastructure:
Internet, Web, and *Net Neutrality*

This chapter gets into the nitty-gritty of how the internet works, so I want to spell out how I'm using the term *infrastructure* and also clarify the difference between the internet and the web. Most people hear the word *infrastructure* and think of things like roads, power cables, and water pipes. They're the physical structures that we need to live in the modern world. But the fact that we rely on these technologies also means we usually forget they're there, like background music or wallpaper. Media theorists Geoffrey Bowker and Susan Leigh Star have argued that infrastructure tends to be invisible until it breaks down, at which point we can't help but notice it. The sudden visibility of infrastructure is obvious to anyone who has gone through a power blackout, had their commute disrupted by a torn-up road, or encountered an out-of-service escalator.

Because we depend on infrastructure in everyday life, its value isn't just technical, it's social. When a technology is baked into our everyday lives, it becomes so essential that it starts to feel like infrastructure. Work, school, dating, banking—for many of us, these activities are so wrapped up in the internet that it's impossible to imagine doing them without digital technologies. At this point, the internet becomes social infrastructure. As tech journalist Mo Lotman observed, "Infrastructure, both social and physical, is built to revolve around our inventions, thereby reinforcing their use and in many cases increasing our dependency." As a result, "we have conditioned ourselves to rely on [digital technologies]." ISPs have a vested interest in keeping their infrastructure off the radar of our collective imagination—it's hard to demand change of technologies that we rely on but can't physically see. It's because the internet has become part of our social infrastructure that we have to think about the politics of its physical infrastructure.

People often use "the internet" and "the web" interchangeably, but they actually refer to different technologies. The internet is the communication network that allows devices to talk to each other. The web is a platform for accessing and sharing content. The internet is older than the web by about twenty years (the internet was invented in 1969, whereas the web was created in 1990). Before the web, people could still communicate and share information by computer, exchanging data and text. What the World Wide Web brought was a public face and access point for online content. We can think of the internet as a group of libraries that share resources with each other, while the web is more like the shelves full of books and media for reading and borrowing. A key difference is that rather than passively accepting what the library puts on the shelves, patrons of the web can add their own content, at any time, with relatively little effort. In chapter 2, I focused mostly on the web. This chapter focuses mostly on the internet, even though many of us experience the internet as a series of web pages and apps. One reason to get specific about the differences between the web and the internet is that they're governed differently. Policies for the web are more or less set by the companies that own the platforms we use. Policies for the internet are determined by a group of international tech organizations, who create standards. Without these standards, the internet would be much more siloed, and entire countries could be disconnected from each other. (Think of the way that countries have their own standards for electrical outlets, which is why you can't plug your Korean laptop into a Canadian outlet without a converter.) And at the national level, federal agencies create policies to monitor ISPs, and by extension the internet. As we'll see, in the United States, these policies have swung back and forth between fostering innovation and protecting corporate profits.

From DIY to Monopoly: The Transformation of ISPs

The question of who controls internet access has always been political. At different times, the internet has been controlled by the military, government agencies, universities, and Big Tech. Each of these stakeholders had different visions and priorities as far as what the internet should do and who it should be for. Since the mid-2000s, the internet's infrastructure has come under the control of major communication and media companies. Comcast, Time Warner Cable, and cell phone carriers like Verizon and AT&T operate as monopolies in huge chunks of the United States. But there was a time when ISPs were small and diverse rather than established megacompanies. As federal regulation has pulled back, the mishmash of ISPs has become much more homogenous and tightly controlled. The big players have gotten bigger, and small players have closed shop. How and why did this happen? What does the commercialization of ISPs mean for ordinary internet users? Tracing this history helps us see the flash points when access to the internet could have been different. (My retelling of this history is going to be on the short side; for more detailed accounts of ISPs and internet history, check out work by Janet Abbate, Kevin Driscoll, Victor Pickard and David Berman, and Megan Sapnar Ankerson, all of which can be found in the references.)

Let's go back to the internet's early days in the 1970s. For cynics and skeptics, the internet's military roots are proof that the technology is inherently violent and controlling. It's true that the internet wouldn't have happened when and how it did without major investments from the U.S. military. While military investment was crucial, the internet wasn't a top-secret, tightly controlled mission like the Manhattan Project or the atomic bomb. From the beginning, the internet involved open collaboration between the government, universities, and industry. As Shane Greenstein explains in his history of the internet, "The military did not take action [on the internet] in an isolated research laboratory. Rather the military funded several inventions, and so did other parts of the government, and so did private industry." In the 1970s, the internet consisted of a small number of hubs operated by the military, government agencies, and universities. Each hub acted as a node in a distributed (but by today's standards, incredibly small) network, and there were several networks operating at the same time. Because protocols were still being worked out, different networks couldn't necessarily talk to each other. When they did talk, communication was limited and only small amounts of data could be transferred. At the time, computers were very expensive and a hassle to move, so an early goal of the internet was sharing computing power. For example, researchers from UCLA could use the internet to communicate with computers at Stanford, linking their terminals to use spare processing time. Email was also an early focus, as were e-mailing lists (aka listservs). There was no web at the time—no browsers or search engines, just computers talking to each other, exchanging messages and data.

In the 1970s and '80s, progress on the internet was steady but slow. New capabilities came from universities as well as private industry. At the time, computer science was still very new as an academic discipline, but from the beginning, it was interdisciplinary and collaborative. Unlike, say, philosophy, it's a field that regularly collaborates with commercial and industry groups. In the 1970s, it was common for computer scientists to move between industry labs and university centers over the course of their careers, and many collaborated with and took funding from the Department of Defense or the Defense Advanced Research Projects Agency, and this is still the case today. These collaborations meant that the internet had a growing number of stakeholders. And the longer the internet was around, the more people realized its potential: the internet wasn't just a telegram that could communicate messages, it was a network that allowed people to share and connect.

As more schools and research hubs linked to the internet, it became clearer that some sort of top-down organization was needed. As a quasi-academic government agency, the NSF was a logical choice. The NSF's main job was managing grants for research across the STEM fields, so it already had a grasp on who was producing cutting-edge tech and a process for managing complex research teams. For most of the 1990s, the NSF managed ISPs. Initially, commercial ISPs were banned, and online access was limited to government agencies and universities. Things changed as the basic operations of the internet stabilized and business opportunities became increasingly obvious. Even with the ban in place, commercial ISPs had started to pop up, although their status was hotly disputed. In 1989, an ISP called the World hooked up its first customer in Brookline, Massachusetts. While some were excited about commercial ISPs expanding access to the internet, many internet hubs blocked or attempted to shut down the World until the NSF finally caved and granted permission to provide public internet access on "an experimental basis." A major turning point came in 1991, when the NSF lifted the ban on commercial ISPs. The World soon had a number of competitors. Barriers to entry for dial-up ISPs were low, and a flood of companies rushed in to bring internet access to ordinary users. For the most part, these companies offered dial-up, using public telephone networks to provide online connection to customers.

Thanks in part to the boom in ISPs, internet use in the United States skyrocketed. In 1996, the entire commercial ISP network in the United States consisted of three thousand ISPs, supplying internet access through 12,000 phone numbers. Two years later, there were 6,000 ISPs working over 65,000 phone numbers. At this point, ISPs offered service to consumers in every major US city. Some of the larger firms started expanding their reach and building national networks. The explosion of URLs gives us another window into the incredible growth of the internet in the 1990s. In September 1995, there were 120,000 registered domain names. Just three years later, the number of registered domain names passed 2 million. That's an 850 percent increase in just three years. As Shane Greenstein explains, "No dramatic technological invention lay behind these changes. Rather a new and stable value chain emerged." According to Greenstein, three factors were driving the expansion of internet access: pricing, infrastructure, and the diversity of ISPs. To break this down, in the 1990s, ISPs discovered it was more profitable to offer a flat rate for unlimited service than to charge customers by the hour (or minute) for internet access. This model required ISPs to boost their abilities to meet growing demands for data. It also became easier and less expensive to build the infrastructure that distributed internet access. And finally, ISPs started to differentiate themselves. Starting in the 1990s, ISPs could be divided into three main groups: backbone providers, national access providers, and local access providers. The first group consisted of private national firms (like MCI, Sprint, UUNET, and BBN), which focused on building the fiber and cable backbone. ISPs in the next two groups were national or local in scale, ranging from wholesale regional firms down to the local ISPs that served small numbers of dial-in customers.

1998 marked the end of NSF's direct role in managing the internet's infrastructure, which then shifted to commercial groups. The number of ISPs reached its peak at just over seven thousand providers in March of 2000. This was a time of incredible choice for consumers. In 1998, more than 92 percent of the U.S. population had access to seven or more ISPs. Fewer than 5 percent lacked access to an ISP. Even then, while there were a lot of ISPs, market share was skewed toward a small number of major providers. According to Greenstein, "A couple dozen of the largest firms accounted for 75 percent of market share nationally and a couple hundred for 90 percent of market share." The majority of ISPs were small dial-ups that covered a small regional area, but the majority of users relied on national providers. Just because ISPs were small didn't mean they all wanted to stay that way. Many ISPs had dreams of expanding to become major players, while others saw their role as a form of community service. Whatever their goals, they created a range of choice and options for consumers.

Over the next thirty years, ISPs consolidated and homogenized. While the 1990s offered consumers and incredible array of choices, by the 2010s, it was a commercialized wasteland. Why did small companies disappear, and how did major providers get so powerful? In the 1990s, it was easy for small start-ups, BBS's, and tech nerds to start an ISP, but it was hard for them to scale up their operations. Meanwhile, television companies and phone carriers already had infrastructure that connected them to customers. And they could offer internet connections at higher speeds. With infrastructure on their side and the government's hands-off approach to regulation, these companies often became the dominant providers.

ISPs have gentrified in the sense that the majority of them used to be more diverse and locally oriented, meeting the needs of a neighborhood or community. But over time, a new model of providing access took hold, displacing smaller, locally focused ISPs. Big providers got bigger, and small providers closed shop. Watching big-scale, national operations replace small-scale start-ups is familiar for people who live in gentrifying neighborhoods. Instead of going to locally owned businesses, money and investment flows to newcomers, who often do a worse job of meeting the needs of longtime residents. Regulatory bodies could have stepped in to protect local ISPs, but instead they sat back and watched as consumer choices dwindled and the corporate power of a small number of players grew. The result is that a tiny number of players wield incredible control over the infrastructure of the internet, with minimal interference from the government and decreased benefits for consumers.

Why does it matter if ISPs have gentrified? According to the FCC, 94 percent of the United States has access to an ISP, so who cares if there's only one provider as long as people can get online? Getting online is one thing. Getting affordable access and having the freedom to choose an ISP that respects privacy is another. Here are the consequences of gentrified infrastructure of the internet: ISPs exploit a lack of competition to price-gouge their consumers, to facilitate government surveillance, and to create profound inequalities of internet access. Let's look at the fallout of ISP gentrification, one issue at a time.

The most obvious result of commercializing ISPs has been a lack of competition. According to a 2015 report by the FCC, just 24 percent of developed areas in the United States have two or more ISPs offering high-speed internet connections. The other 76 percent are left with a single provider, which drives up costs for consumers and hinders innovation. The commercialization of online access has culminated in an ISP juggernaut that's perfectly okay with leaving some people behind as long as wealthy folks in accessible neighborhoods continue to sign up for contracts. This model of commercialization is a familiar pattern in gentrifying neighborhoods, where new businesses market themselves to buyers with the most money, pushing out older businesses and excluding people on the margins.

The lack of ISP competition also has frightening implications for our individual privacy. In 2017, the U.S. Senate voted along party lines to repeal Obama-era privacy protections. As a result, ISPs can now collect data on consumer browsing habits. As we saw in chapter 2, data brokers are middlemen between tech companies and advertisers, and they want information about users in order to generate revenue through targeted ads. Without competition for internet access, consumers are forced to give their business to companies that don't protect individual privacy. An article by the foundation Skycoin explains the situation:

> Imagine the Post Office being permitted to read every letter you send without your consent. All users who aren't employing privacy-protecting tools like VPNs will be subject to their website browsing history and all unsecured traffic being harvested and sold by their ISP. . . . Not only are US citizens paying exorbitant fees to corporate ISPs for internet access, they are also paying to have their browsing habits harvested, sent to the central US surveillance apparatus and mined by their ISP for marketing purposes.

It isn't just that some ISPs got big in the 2010s and some ISPs died, it's that the business model of a successful ISP became less experimental and more exploitative.

What kinds of data are ISPs taking from their users? A report from the Center for Digital Democracy found that major ISPs like Comcast, Cox Communications, Time Warner Cable, and Verizon collect information about income, education level, and purchase behavior from consumers. Advertisers can purchase this data in order to sell, for example, high-interest credit cards and loan offers to consumers in debt. The same report found that Verizon offers advertisers "targeting packages" geared toward low-income communities. These packages push ads for gambling, cigarettes, and soda toward poor folks, which is a key way that privacy harms are more skewed toward people on the margins. Tamika Lewis, Seeta Peña Gangadharan, Mariella Saba, and Tawana Petty, the group of digital privacy activists behind the project Our Data Bodies, explain that data brokers have serious privacy implications for all of us, but "for marginalized and vulnerable citizens the buying and selling of our information by data brokers also ties to problems of predatory targeting, racial profiling, and discrimination by the state and corporations alike."

There's a third way that the ISP monopoly hurts consumers, which has to do with geography and isolation. We like to think of the internet as a technology that overcomes spatial distance. It's true that the internet can connect people across the globe instantaneously, but geography still matters when it comes to digital infrastructure, because where someone lives has a lot to do with how many choices they have as far as providers. People in urban areas and rich neighborhoods tend to have more ISPs to choose from than people in poor and rural areas. ISPs have a name for the difficulty involved in getting access to everyone: the last mile problem. Cable companies have invested billions of dollars in copper and fiber optics, stretching across the country. The cables connect exchange nodes to individual households. This distance between the hub and the residential or commercial access points is referred to as the "last mile." By controlling the last mile, ISPs have the final say about which businesses, homes, and neighborhoods get access and which ones are left out.

Higher costs, hypercommercialization, and increased inequality—the harms of the ISP monopoly have key parallels in gentrifying neighborhoods. From this perspective, ISPs have become the Walmart of internet infrastructure. Their main appeal is that they're accessible and able to offer the lowest common denominator of products. They provide essentials but displace locally owned shops. Sociologists and economists have found that when Walmart opens up a new store, it's mostly bad for low-income neighborhoods. Before long, Walmart puts local shops out of business while providing fewer choices at higher costs (not to mention, they're usually unsympathetic employers). And that's also what we see with the consolidated ISP market: displacement of local businesses, higher costs, and poorer services.

How can we tackle the problem of ISP monopolies? Like urban gentrification, one key element for dealing with gentrified infrastructure is regulation. Policy decisions could place caps on fees and charges, issue a consumer bill of rights, and ensure accountability. So what would it take to start regulating ISPs and enforcing a level playing field? Enter net neutrality. Net neutrality has become the main rallying point for internet activists who worry that the internet will become less open and more commercial without regulation. At the most basic level, net neutrality is about guaranteeing equal access to the internet. It's the belief that ISPs should treat all content routed through their cables and cell towers the same. The term comes from Tim Wu, a law professor who was concerned by how much power ISPs had over ordinary internet users. Net neutrality is meant to make sure that ISPs don't upcharge customers based on the services they use, by basically forcing ISPs to treat customers equally regardless of the sites and platforms they visit. As Klint Finley explains in *Wired*, "That means [ISPs] shouldn't be able to slide some data into 'fast lanes' while blocking or otherwise discriminating against other material." Speeding up and slowing down web content isn't just inconvenient, it's harmful. Public debate and an open internet are at stake here. Writing about net neutrality and media policy, Victor Pickard and David Berman argue that "allowing ISPs to divide the internet into fast and slow lanes will inevitably amplify the voices, ideas and worldviews of those with power and resources, while marginalizing those without them."

Without net neutrality laws, there's nothing to stop providers from charging people who use a particular service, like Zoom, more or from slowing down Netflix or Hulu. That's the consumer side of net neutrality. On the media company side, a broadband provider could play favorites with content platforms by allowing companies to pay more in exchange for priority treatment. Over time, companies and organizations that can't afford to pay for priority treatment, or just aren't offered a deal by ISPs, would effectively be left behind by the mainstream web.

Net neutrality and urban gentrification share some key themes and drivers: concerns about inequality, displacement, and isolation. Left unregulated, ISPs could displace or isolate both people and platforms. They also share a solution: government regulation. Both the George W. Bush and Obama administrations offered some support for net neutrality through the FCC. Broadband providers won a number of legal battles on the issue during the first decade of the twenty-first century, before the FCC finally passed sweeping net neutrality protections in 2015. But things shifted again with the election of Donald Trump in 2016. In December of 2017, the Republican-controlled FCC voted to undo Obama-era legislation, freeing broadband providers to block or throttle content as they see fit. In general, Big Tech is wary of regulation, but net neutrality sets up a battle between major industry players. On one side, you have Verizon and Comcast pushing an antiregulation agenda. On the other, Google, Netflix, Microsoft, and many other companies have come out in support of net neutrality, fearing that they could be charged more or risk having their content slowed down. If ISPs weren't such a monopoly, net neutrality wouldn't be so worrisome. With real competition, ISPs would have to fight for customers, which would lower costs and spur innovation. As it is, customers have to fight for choice. Net neutrality activists are working for increased accountability and consumer advocacy. They're also trying to keep the internet's infrastructure on a level playing field. While ISP regulation swings back and forth at the FCC, activists are reimagining what online access and digital connection might look like.

The Radical Democracy of Mesh Networks

How could we decommercialize and diversify the internet's infrastructure? What are the alternatives to ISPs? Looking to take back control over the means of connection, activists around the world are turning to mesh networking, or meshnets. Traditionally, ISPs provide a household with an access point to the internet by plugging a house or apartment into a network. Meshnets work differently. Rather than connecting via a single point of entry controlled by an ISP, meshnets rely on a shared connection spread out among dozens or even hundreds of wireless mesh nodes. Each node in a meshnet "talks" to the others, collectively supporting a network connection. A technical difference in these two models is that mesh networks are truly wireless. Traditional wireless access means that laptops and phones don't need to be physically plugged into a network, but the router has to have a physical connection to a hub, which usually means that Ethernet cables need to be buried in ceilings and walls. In a wireless mesh network, only one node has to be linked to a network connection, and then that one wired node shares its internet connection with other nodes close by. The more nodes, the further the connection spreads, creating a network of connectivity that can scale throughout a small office or across a city of millions.

In terms of power dynamics, the key difference between meshnets and traditional ISPs comes down to ownership. ISPs either rent or control internet cable, apartment by apartment and house by house. Meshnets can distribute internet access without adding additional fiber or cable. The technology behind meshnets is fairly straightforward, which gives activist and community groups a lot of control over their operation. Users can get online access for little or no cost, with the added benefit of increased security against corporate surveillance. Meshnets can make good on the democratic rhetoric of the early internet, at least as far as putting tools of online access into individual hands. At the same time, there's nothing inherently liberatory about meshnets. Mainstream ISPs also offer mesh technologies to increase coverage throughout a house or office. Depending on who's building them, meshnets can either extend or disrupt ISP power.

Mesh networks offer more security and local control of the network. But they also come with drawbacks. The main issue is meeting users' ever-increasing appetite for data. Today's mesh networks would have worked great for yesterday's internet users. But in a moment where many people have multiple devices and are constantly streaming content, mesh networks struggle to provide enough bandwidth. Meshnets work better in some settings than others. The need for interlinked nodes means that meshnets are more feasible in high-density populations. Mesh networks have also been criticized for reproducing rather than undoing inequality. Although meshnets have a loyal DIY following, there's still a hurdle of technical know-how, which sets up inequalities around race, class, and gender. It also takes a degree of privilege and stability to build a stable mesh network. Participation can make more sense for home owners than renters, and the taller the house, the better. Finally, there's nothing to guarantee that a mesh network will be used to make the internet fairer rather than more dangerous. Criminal organizations and cyber terrorists can benefit from mesh networks as much as the communities ignored by commercial ISPs.

The limitations of meshnets matter. But they shouldn't keep us from thinking about when and how mesh networks could be part of the solution to ISP gentrification. At the very least, meshnets increase awareness about the internet's infrastructure. And at the most, meshnets could upend a powerful ISP monopoly that restricts online access.

Activist groups around the world are using mesh networks to increase security—and to protest the control of ISPs. For example, Brooklyn's Red Hook WiFi is a "community-led effort to close the digital divide." Located in southwestern Brooklyn, Red Hook is cut off from the rest of the borough by an expressway and poorly served by public transport. It's also poorly served by ISPs, in part because of its geography and in part because many of its residents are low-income. Convinced that meshnets could increase access to the internet, Red Hook Initiative installed a mesh network of wireless nodes in the neighborhood in 2012. Later that year, Hurricane Sandy crashed through New York, and Red Hook was hit particularly hard. At a moment when big chunks of the city were without power and underwater, Red Hook meshnets allowed local residents to communicate with each other about their status and needs. As a measure of the project's value to the community, Red Hook Initiative has been invited to advise New York City Mayor Bill de Blasio's efforts to bring Wi-Fi to the city's public housing.

Over in Oakland, California, People's Open offers a West Coast version of community-owned and operated wireless networks. People's Open builds and operates wireless mesh networks in cooperation with local neighborhoods. It also "provide[s] open source software, off-the-shelf hardware, and educational materials used to host workshops, train operators, and install nodes." The network has over forty nodes in the San Francisco Bay Area, and People's Open is currently working on building access to gigabits of donated bandwidth and connecting a homeless camp in Berkeley.

It's not a coincidence that some of the cities most affected by gentrification are also hotspots of meshnet activities. Brooklyn and Oakland are both epicenters of gentrification. For a long time, Red Hook was protected from the gentrification seizing Brooklyn because it's far away from the subway. It's also home to a lot of public housing (More than half of Red Hook's twelve thousand residents are tenants of the New York City Housing Authority), which scares off some developers and gentrifiers. But with real estate developers gobbling up more and more parts of Brooklyn, gentrification has slowly taken over Red Hook. In 2006, a chain grocery store opened up in the area, which kicked off a wave of development. A private school popped up (with a tuition of $30,200 a year) and abandoned warehouses were transformed into luxury condos. Similar transformations are taking place in Oakland. Between 1990 and 2000, less than 3 percent of Oakland's neighborhoods were gentrified. Between 2000 and 2013, that number climbed to 30 percent. Meshnets are a response to the last mile problem and mass displacement of local ISPs. They're also a response to gentrification. In communities where businesses and housing are skewed toward people of privilege, developing resources to meet local needs becomes a form of activism. Meshnets offer a different model of commercialization, one that's responsive to the needs of local community.

From a technical perspective, mesh networks are a radical shift in online connectivity. The meshnet model is built on collective participation instead of corporate consolidation. Rather than relying on a small number of ISPs for online access, mesh networks rely on the cooperation of people who turn their homes or offices or rooftops into network nodes. From an activist perspective, anything that disrupts the monopoly of ISPs is a good thing. Simply by providing an alternative for getting online, meshnets help address the internet's hypercommercialism. But there's another way that mesh networks help address technological inequality, which is that they force us to think more concretely about infrastructure. Learning what a meshnet is and how to install it means getting familiar with the infrastructure of the internet and its politics. Meshnets are also fundamentally collective, a literal example of the internet's democratic potential.

Whose Cables? Our Cables! The Activist Promise of Dark Fiber

There's another radical possibility for taking back control of the internet's infrastructure. Rather than building their own networks, activists could take over fiber that's already been laid down but never been turned on. Media theorist Germaine Haleguoa has investigated these networks of dark fiber, or "fiber optic cables that are buried under streets and sidewalks but remain unlit. Since there is no light pulsing through the cable, no data can be transmitted, therefore the cables are 'off' or inactive." How did these miles of excess fiber come to be, and why haven't they been turned on? In the late 1990s, cable companies overinvested in digital infrastructure. Spurred by serious cyber-hype, companies laid down miles of fiber and built new long-haul backbone networks. Then came the tech bubble burst, followed by a wave of bankruptcies and liquidations. But the fiber was still there, often getting bought and sold without ever being turned on. In other cases, companies deliberately kept dark fiber turned off to limit consumer choices. But dark fiber networks are still usable, and most of them are still for sale. In many cities, dark fiber is available and totally capable of bringing internet access to thousands of homes. ISPs can light up dark fiber and extend them for residential, commercial, or government use. But instead of adding competition to the ISP market and meeting the needs of underserved neighborhoods, miles and miles of dark fiber sits unleased and unused.

Some cities in the United States (including Roanoke, Virginia; Huntsville, Alabama; and Centennial, Colorado) have started experimenting with "open access" dark fiber networks to promote local investment and competition among ISPs. But there's a more radical way that we could go about reusing this infrastructure, following in the path of activists who reclaim infrastructure. From the Native Americans occupation of Alcatraz to punk squats across Europe, activist history has many examples of finding ways to repurpose abandoned or unused infrastructure. Could internet activists find a way to gain local control over dark fiber?

Dark fiber activism could follow in the path of public TV and community radio. In the United States, hundreds of public access television production facilities were launched in the 1970s. The FCC required major market cable systems to offer three access channels, one each for public, educational, and local government use. In 1976, the rule was upgraded to adapt to cable. In communities with 3,500 or more subscribers, cable companies were required to set aside cable TV channels for use by the public. In 1984, Congress passed the Cable Act, which essentially gave cable providers the ability to opt out of the requirements to protect public channels. (The federal government's failure to protect consumer choice and decision to side instead with media companies should feel familiar after learning about the FCC and net neutrality.) But public television endures in cities like New York, Boston, Chicago, and Philadelphia, as well as in a number of smaller markets, like the Tri Valley in California and Fairfax, Virginia.

Public access TV follows in the footsteps of public radio. Since the 1930s, congressional and FCC policies have mandated that radio spectrum be set aside for noncommercial use. The FCC first began reserving spectrum for noncommercial, educational radio broadcast use in 1938. The FCC continues to reserve the lowest twenty channels on the FM broadcast band for educational purposes. In her book on community radio activism, Christina Dunbar-Hester describes the activist commitments to radio as local media.

Dunbar-Hester documented the challenges of overcoming racial and gendered discrimination around access to tech but ultimately found that local radio could be a powerful tool for social justice and community solidarity. Dark fiber activists could build a similar case for demanding that the FCC reserve a portion of dark fiber for noncommercial and educational access to the internet. This is a more radical vision than the current experiments in cities like Roanoke and Centennial, where the idea is to increase the number of ISPs rather than challenge mainstream models of the commercialized internet.

Community land trusts are another model of local ownership that could be useful for activist repurposing of dark fiber. Community land trusts purchase local properties and hold them "in trust." They can then be sold, at below market rates, to local community members who might not be able to afford homes at market rates. Community land trusts keep neighborhoods affordable by retaining ownership of the land and having decisions driven by the community. For example, Philadelphia's Community Justice Land Trust got its start in 1986 as the Women's Community Revitalization Project, the city's first and only women-led community development organization. Since then, the organization has grown and built just under three hundred units of housing. The activist power of community-owned land trusts is that control over neighborhood housing and resources comes from inside the community. As nonprofits and community-based organizations, community land trusts are less impacted by local changes to the real estate market. Activist groups could adopt a similar model for ownership over dark fiber. By pooling resources, local communities that aren't being served by major ISPs could take over dark fiber, increasing competition and experimenting with both nonprofit and commercial models. This would require active stewardship from activist groups and local industry, but it wouldn't require building anything new, just taking control of something that's not being used and handing it over to people who have been left behind in the gentrification of digital infrastructure.

Rather than resorting to a capitalist's solution to a capitalism problem, I'm calling for the redistribution of unused (but usable!) infrastructure. I'm not saying we have to choose between mesh-nets and dark fiber, or that these approaches can work for every internet user in every city. Depending on where someone lives, one of these approaches may work better than the other. In many cases, they could be used together to provide a more robust set of options for getting different people with different needs online. The compelling thing about both of these approaches is that they push back on the gentrification of the internet's infrastructure.

It's easy to feel defeatist about the practicalities of changing infrastructure. Individual people can't build high-speed fiber networks, and the companies in play are huge, wealthy, and powerful. I get the skepticism, but there are important examples of activists demanding—and getting—massive changes in infrastructure. Prior to the 1960s, people with disabilities struggled for participation and visibility in everyday life. Buildings weren't wheelchair accessible, mainstream media was inaccessible to the blind and deaf, and people with intellectual disabilities or neuroatypical disorders had no protections from discrimination in the classroom or workplace. Politicians met their demands for accessibility with skepticism—it would simply cost too much to charge infrastructure. But disability activists pushed back, occupying buildings in San Francisco and staging demonstrations in Washington, D.C. After a steady campaign of direct action and coalition building, they won major victories at the federal level. A crucial part of the activists' strategy was creating a wide coalition. They brought together people with learning disabilities and degenerative conditions, people with hearing and vision impairments, people who used wheelchairs, canes, and walkers, and people who experienced many other forms of disability. After working tirelessly for decades, disability activists led a transformation in how buildings are built, how sidewalks are shaped, and how government messages are broadcast. These transformations didn't happen overnight, and minds didn't change out of nowhere. Things changed because of hard work, multiple arrests, and serious personal risk by activists who insisted that infrastructure was political.

The ISPs we have weren't inevitable, and they aren't invincible. They can be challenged and forced to change. While federal regulation is an important tool in taking back control of the internet's infrastructure, we should also demand change at the local level. Cities and neighborhoods could embrace partnerships with local meshnet groups and explore dark fiber options. Like all corporations, ISPs win when consumers believe there are no alternatives. And that means that the biggest threat to ISPs and the best way to push back on gentrifying infrastructure is to build and reclaim alternative paths to digital connection.

5   *Resistance*

If I've done my job right, at this point you should have a clear sense of what gentrification means and how it describes the mainstream internet. You might also be feeling a sense of frustration—or fatigue. Fueled by controversies like the Cambridge Analytica scandal, global concerns about election interference, and the seemingly endless list of tech industry screwups, techno-skepticism is gaining in popularity. By techno-skepticism, I mean the belief that new technologies are more likely to be manipulative and disempowering than democratic and equitable. In a lot of ways, techno-skepticism is a reasonable response to privacy fails and the constant feed of scandals in Big Tech. There's even a magazine called *Techno Skeptic,* and it's no surprise that its editor, Mo Lotman, takes issue with the idea that technology is a reliable path toward empowerment, asking, if technologies empower us, "how can they also be inevitable and unstoppable? . . . Either technologies are inherently empowering, in which case we should be empowered to choose what to adopt, . . . or some technologies, at least, are disempowering and controlling."

A bit of skepticism can be helpful when we think about technology. A lot of promises have been made about the digital path to democracy and equality, most of which have not been fulfilled. As Alexis Madrigal lamented in an article for the *Atlantic*, "People were railroaded into a few platforms of enormous power, fed into enormous surveillance machines, mined for attention, guided by algorithms, all while they contributed to the radical inequality of the broader society." With increasing levels of corporate and government surveillance on top of the parade of Big Tech failures, it's hard not to get cynical. We've seen a familiar cycle where a controversy provokes outrage, companies express regret and announce minor policy changes, and then we all go back to using and being used by social media. But skepticism won't help us build a better internet. To echo Tamika Lewis, Seeta Peña Gangadharan, Mariella Saba, Tawana Petty, the activists behind Our Data Bodies, the goal should be "to ensure that we are leaving our community members with a sense of power, not paranoia." What's needed is more rights for users and more ways to turn feelings of skepticism and paranoia into a sense of power.

The biggest weapon that Big Tech has is the widespread belief that it's too big to fail and too successful to challenge. The tech industry has a lot of resources and political power, and its products touch every part of our lives. But tech companies need us more than we need them. Their business models depend on our attention, content, and data. If we want a fairer, better internet, we have to demand change from our platforms—and each other. We have to find ways to build coalitions, get involved in policy decisions, and demand more accountability.

What would degentrifying the internet look like? And what are the next steps to get there? Much like Big Tech, gentrification can feel like an overwhelming, unstoppable force. But there are success stories in the battle to keep city space diverse. We can learn from these actions and borrow tactics in the fight for a fairer internet. The agenda I outline here is partly inspired by activists fighting gentrification in their neighborhoods. I'll also pull in ideas from privacy activists and design justice groups who are committed to more freedom and inclusion online. An anti-gentrification action plan doesn't need to have an end game of toppling Facebook or tearing down infrastructure. It just has to show us legitimate alternatives to the web we have now and a plan for how to get more accountability from users, platforms, and policymakers.

Who are these tactics for? Is this kind of activism just for people who've been excluded and marginalized by Big Tech? Or to put it another way, if gentrifiers are part of the problem, can they also be part of the solution? I believe that Big Tech and people of privilege have to be part of the response to a gentrifying internet. That means pushing back on problems that have already surfaced and working to prevent similar issues from occurring in the future. In any kind of social justice activism, allyship has to be part of the equation, otherwise, it's people on the margins who are going to have to keep doing all the work. It's the job of antiracist White people to convince other White folks not to be racist, the job of feminist men to convince other men not to be sexist, the job of straight and cis allies work against homophobia and transphobia. In cities, the antigentrification movement can't be limited to people whose homes are on the line. It has to offer a path for newcomers to be better neighbors. Online, the call to fight gentrification has to protect communities that want to preserve their culture, and it also has to chart a course for gentrified platforms to become more open and inclusive.

Urban Gentrification: What Does Resistance Look Like?

Gentrification is a global problem, but the toll it takes is specific to each neighborhood. It makes sense, then, that pushing back against gentrification looks different from city to city. I want to take us on a tour of antigentrification activism with two goals in mind: to remind ourselves that change is possible, even when gentrification seems like an unstoppable force, and to figure out what tactics of antigentrification activists can be mapped onto struggles for a fairer internet.

In 2004, tenants of East Harlem formed a group called the Movement for Justice in El Barrio (MJB). The driving force for the group was fighting gentrification in a neighborhood known for Latino and Black culture and heritage. In 2007, the British firm Dawnay Day Group bought forty-seven buildings in the area. At the time, Dawnay Day Group's director, Phil Blakeley, made no secret of his plans for the buildings, saying the company is doing its part to "bring along Harlem's gentrification," as reported by Michael Gould-Wartofsky in *Counterpunch*. MJB organized demonstrations at city hall and organized tenant committees. The tenant committees demanded better conditions in neglected buildings and launched a lawsuit against Dawnay Day for "illegal harassment." Dawnay Day went bankrupt during the 2008 recession, but even with the investors gone, MJB had work to do. With properties in limbo, tenants were still living in terrible conditions, without a process for voicing concerns and demanding repairs. In 2010, MBJ's lawsuit was decided in their favor. Activist and journalist Annie Correal described the important rights won by tenants: a guarantee that buildings would not revert to the previous mismanaged owners and assurances that "the tenants have access to all the accounts of how the administration is using the money and . . . have rights to take the administration to the Housing Court for repairs." In the end, MJB was able to build a lasting process for demanding change, giving local people a voice in what happened in their neighborhood.

In chapter 3, we saw how Big Tech is changing San Francisco's cultural geography. So it's no surprise that the Bay Area has also produced major antigentrification activism. In 2013, a San Francisco antigentrification group called Heart of the City began a series of protests. They focused on the private buses that transport Big Tech employees to the South Bay. Companies like Apple, Facebook, Genentech, and Google all use private transit arrangements as perks for their employees. Writer Rebecca Solnit described the buses as a blatant symbol of inequality:

> The buses roll up to San Francisco's bus stops in the morning and evening, but they are unmarked, or nearly so, and not for the public. They have no signs or have discreet acronyms on the front windshield, and because they also have no rear doors they ingest and disgorge their passengers slowly, while the brightly lit funky orange public buses wait behind them. The luxury coach passengers ride for free and many take out their laptops and begin their work day on board; there is of course Wi-Fi. Most of them are gleaming white, with dark-tinted windows, like limousines.

Solnit's image is one of privilege and isolation, of mobile filter bubbles that allow tech sector employees to avoid confrontations with local people. For weeks, Heart of the City blocked and boarded the buses, which they saw as "symbols of deeper problems: a gaping wealth divide, worsening housing crisis and rampant displacement." Protesters put infrastructure at the center of their protests, posing as construction workers with signs reading "Warning: Illegal use of public infrastructure." The group also wrote and distributed a fake city ordinance that outlined a vision for what the city should do. At the top of their list was the demand that the tech companies who hired the shuttles pay to use public infrastructure for private purposes. The protests ultimately forced the city to institute a new set of regulatory laws called the Commuter Shuttle Program in 2016, which forced the bus companies to pay the city for the usage of the bus stops.

Gentrification happens in partnership with local governments and the blessing of local regulation. So it makes sense that antigentrification work can use the same levers of local laws and policies. After years of booming real estate, Miami took a policy approach to slow down gentrification. Local legislators changed the rules for regulating building height, allowing the city to grow vertically.[1] Assuming that demand for property would keep increasing in Miami, city policymakers saw building upward as their best bet to prevent the "spillover of the banking class" into historic neighborhoods like Little Havana, according to urban policy journalist Scott

---

1. Climate change is a major threat to the city of Miami. While building upward may have an impact on gentrification, it's also a policy that ignores a looming environmental crisis. It's beyond the scope of this book to get into the connections between gentrification and climate change. But I do want to say that I'm conflicted about using Miami's local policy as an activist blueprint, even though it's an important example of how cities are experimenting with local laws to combat gentrification.

Beyer. Montreal took a different approach to fighting gentrification by using zoning laws. In 2016, the city passed a bylaw preventing new restaurants from opening up within twenty-five feet of an existing restaurant. As one of the lawmakers behind the bill explained, "Residents need to be able to have access to a range of goods and services within walking distance of their homes. Lots of restaurants are fine and dandy, but we also need grocery stores, bakeries and retail spaces" (as reported by Matthew Hays in the *Guardian*). The rule protects longtime establishments and encourages commercial diversity. Confronting a demand for new housing and new restaurants, Miami and Montreal turned zoning laws into tools for protecting local communities.

In Chicago, Paseo Boricua has long been home to a vibrant Puerto Rican community. The neighborhood has been battling gentrification since the 1990s. Local community groups have focused their efforts on economic development and local businesses that reproduce Puerto Rican culture. Paseo Boricua is located within the Humboldt Park Redevelopment Area (HPRA), which was created in 1994 to shape business development within the frameworks of local community organizations. According to urban studies research Ivis Garcia, part of HPRA's strength came from its incredible commitment to coalition building—the group brought together more than eighty community groups. Emphasizing the neighborhood's Puerto Rican roots, HPRA was able to recruit new, locally owned businesses to the area. Their recruitment efforts included a commitment to different kinds of businesses that could appeal to consumers with diverse income levels. Planners also focused on providing spaces rooted in Puerto Rican and Latino culture and spaces that weren't just for shopping but hanging out.

Puerto Rican residents started to invest in the area, rehabilitating building façades and undertaking major renovations. By pooling their resources and influence, local residents were able to take more control over the kinds of businesses that could open in their neighborhood.

These are some of the ways that local activists are pushing back on urban gentrification. What are the takeaways for the struggle for a fairer internet? As we saw in MJB's battle over East Harlem, sometimes legal action is necessary. And so is focusing on the process of speaking back to power. Puerto Ricans in Paseo Boricua were able to gain more control over their neighborhood because they built community organizations that bought, sold, and developed homes and businesses. MJB activists also focused on creating structures—like tenant committees—to give residents a voice in what happened in their buildings and neighborhood. We can't just wait for a recession to wipe out property developers (and as we saw in the 2008 recession, sometimes economic downturns just open the door to more gentrification). But we can take legal action with clear goals, like increased transparency and accountability.

Antigentrification activism also shows us the need for action at multiple levels: legal action, corporate pressure, demands for local legislation, and direct action. Tech companies are susceptible to pressure, but getting them to change requires collective organization and community action. Without Heart of the City, tech companies might never have had to pay up for using public infrastructure for private gains. Regulation is also key to antigentrification projects, as we saw in Miami and Montreal. Local legislation doesn't just randomly happen, it takes pressure from residents who push for change.

A Toolkit for Fighting Back against the Gentrification of the Internet

Just as there's no one-size-fits-all answer for cities who want to limit gentrification, a multipurpose toolkit is needed for agitating against isolation, displacement, and commercialization online. Different tactics are required to push back on a gentrifying internet. Not all of them draw directly on urban antigentrification work, but they share a commitment to a multifaceted effort to fight for a better, fairer internet. At the back of this book, along with a glossary and a list of references, I've included a list of activist groups committed to net neutrality and pushing back on digital discrimination. Supporting and learning from these groups can be an important first step toward building another, better internet.

Be your own algorithm. Rather than passively accepting the networks and content that platforms feed us, we need to take more ownership over what our networks look like. As users, we can take small steps to diversify our online content. Part of the convenience and entertainment offered by social media platforms is that they deliver content. Algorithms sort through our updates, photos, videos, and links to create personalized feeds that keep us up to date and entertained. Like most algorithms, the formulas driving our social media feeds can be useful. They push new content from people in our networks, keeping us in the loop with what's going on with folks we know. But while feeds are convenient for users, they're also limiting. They're motivated not by helping us learn but by making money for companies. Feeds are designed to keep us online for as long as possible—in order to show us as many ads as possible.

Platforms like Facebook and YouTube have tweaked their algorithms for recommended content because they've been pressured over facilitating the spread of viral news and extreme content. The 2020 global pandemic of COVID-19 reminded us of the need for platforms to monitor content. In the midst of so much uncertainty about how the virus spreads and what local resources were available, Facebook and YouTube struggled to combat hoaxes, scams, and misinformation. Under pressure from journalists, policymakers, health care professionals, and concerned users, platforms banned ads and posts that "directly result in physical harm." Misinformation doesn't spread just because people share it, it spreads because algorithms push content that echoes rather than argues with our views. We should keep calling out social media companies that place ad revenue over public health and personal well-being. But as platforms continue to tweak their formulas, we can take steps to be our own algorithms and deliberately diversify our networks and the content we see.

On a practical level, this means doing an audit of the people we follow and asking, How can I diversify these voices and perspectives? This might mean seeking out more POC, women, queer folk, differently abled people, or neuroatypical people, or it might mean trying to expose ourselves to content from people with different political views, who live in different parts of the country or different parts of the world. Shaking up our networks can create more awareness about how platforms operate, giving us a clearer sense of a platform's priorities. It can also push back against the segregation and filter bubbles of online platforms. By being our own algorithms and leaning in to diversity, we can reclaim some of the early web hype about encountering new people and learning new perspectives.

We need new narratives of success in Big Tech. In chapter 4, I talked about how the success of Big Tech is always measured in dollars.

The same priorities dominate the landscape of a gentrified neighborhood. We need to start pushing different stories of what a successful tech company looks like. Enough with the feel-good stories of Googlers who volunteer on the weekends or one-off donations from Big Tech executives to charitable causes. We need social media companies that embrace new business models and new definitions of success. Some of the pressure to reform Big Tech is already coming from inside the industry. As described in chapter 3, more and more tech workers are producing their own grassroots narrations of Big Tech. They're writing open letters to company leadership, organizing walkouts, and in some cases, unionizing. We need to support efforts from within Big Tech for fairness and inclusion, which could take the form of online boycotts or media campaigns. Remembering angry Tumblr users who threatened to hold their attention hostage to preserve their online norms, we have to recognize our own value to Big Tech. At that point, we can also imagine—and demand—new narratives from Big Tech.

Your convenience isn't worth more than someone else's safety. Is safety a right or a privilege? And when does feeling safe come at the expense of someone else's rights? Online privacy is increasingly something people pay for, whether it's by using premium streaming services to avoid ads or shelling out for antivirus protection. But often, the people who need the most protection are those who can least afford it. Levels of online harassment are much, much higher for women, POC, and LGBT folks. These groups are much more likely to be trolled, doxed (have their private information posted publicly), or swatted (a high-stakes prank that involves making a fake bomb threat that results in law enforcement showing up at a target's house). Even in cases where people aren't physically attacked, online harassment takes a huge toll on the victim's mental health, and it can make our online publics less diverse when historically marginalized groups are afraid to speak up out of fear.

Both online and off, race and class have a lot to do with who's perceived as a threat. As online platforms gentrify, they can exclude or discriminate against people on the margins. But the link between gentrification and jeopardizing the well-being of others through technology can also be direct and literal. For example, Our Data Bodies activists connected gentrifiers' concerns over safety to technology that harms communities of color: "For undocumented, black communities and other marginalized communities, the safer a city proposes to be, the less safe those communities become. When cities invest in the security of neighborhoods by adding surveillance cameras and increasing the militarization of police departments, it poses an imminent threat to those residents who are often deemed expendable. The security mindset without [a] human element is inherently unsafe."

Products that promise safety can create outsized consequences for people who have a lot to lose. Take the issue of package pirates, or people who steal packages that have been left in mailboxes and at front doors. It can be frustrating or scary to have stuff stolen from your front door. But keeping our mail safe shouldn't be the excuse for partnerships between gentrification, local police, and Big Tech. In gentrifying neighborhoods, home security devices are regularly installed in flipped houses and new builds. In some cities, the tech companies behind these devices work hand in hand with local police forces. Writing for the *Atlantic,* Lauren Smiley described how Amazon is helping police departments run "bait box" operations, where police put decoy boxes with GPS trackers inside on random porches. If someone takes the bait, police swoop in to make an arrest. Theft is a crime, but we should weigh whether stolen Amazon packages (which the company will almost certainly replace for free) are worth inviting police surveillance into our homes and turning it on our neighbors. This is especially worth considering in gentrifying neighborhoods, where mostly wealthy and White residents are working with Big Tech and local police to monitor poorer neighbors. When companies promise us safety through digital technology, we should remember to ask, Whose safety? How do the devices and technologies we use affect the people around us? As Our Data Bodies activists argued, we should aim for technologies that look more like porch lights and less like home alarm systems. Alarm systems are meant to protect a family, but porch lights are meant to protect a neighborhood.

In the city, as online, we need regulation. As activists at the LA Tenants Union remind us, "We don't have a housing crisis. We have a tenants' rights crisis." Just like activists are struggling to work with lawmakers to increase tenants' rights, internet users are struggling to find political allies to intervene in Silicon Valley. Time and again, tech company executives are called to testify before government officials (in the United States and elsewhere), but this doesn't seem to produce real change in how platforms operate. It certainly doesn't affect their profit margins. In 2018, Mark Zuckerberg testified before the U.S. Congress after it came out that Facebook had allowed a political consultancy group called Cambridge Analytica to access over eighty-seven million user accounts. After the story broke, Facebook's stock tumbled by $37 billion. During Zuckerberg's testimony, investors were so comforted by his responses—and the obvious reluctance of politicians to regulate Big Tech—that Facebook's stock surged. By testifying for a few hours, Zuckerberg earned his company $21 billion. Facebook shares went up 4.5 percent to $165 from $157.93 the day before—it was the company's most significant one-day gain in about two years. And as a major shareholder, Zuckerberg increased his own wealth by $3 billion. Rather than getting accountability from Facebook or regulation from lawmakers, the main outcome from Zuckerberg's testimony was an increase in Facebook's stock value.

In cities, gentrification is bigger than the decisions of a few people about where to live—it requires active support of local governments. Or to put it another way, one of the most important tools of resisting gentrification is local housing and zoning policy. When local policymakers give tax breaks to developers, people are incentivized to flip houses and build massive apartment complexes, displacing local people. There's a big financial incentive for urban developers to figure out how to make local regulation work to their advantage. The same thing happens in the tech industry, which hires lobbyists to sway federal legislation. Tech companies are increasingly pouring money into lobbying the federal government. Amazon, Apple, Facebook, and Google spent a combined $55 million on lobbying in 2018, doubling their combined spending of $27.4 million in 2016. But as we saw in Miami and Montreal, policymakers can also make rules that slow down gentrification or lessen its impact.

We need to demand intervention from lawmakers on net neutrality, user privacy, and online harassment. And that starts with learning the local landscape of internet infrastructure. How many ISPs are there in your neighborhood? Are there small providers or mesh network alternatives? How about dark fiber? How many of your local representatives accept donations from major internet providers like Comcast? Start with your congressperson or city council rep, both of whom will likely have staffers who answer the phone rather than kicking you to a message machine. Ask about their position on net neutrality, about internet penetration, about local support for digital media literacy. Being informed is a crucial step in understanding the barriers to radical change.

The call to reach out to government officials can feel deflating. That's *all* we're supposed to do? Reach out to our representatives? Calling representatives can't be our only response—we also have to make different decisions as consumers and join actions like protests, marches, and boycotts. But learning the ins and outs of issues and contacting politicians *can* make a difference. In my experience, calling representatives keeps me informed about what a politician is doing and why. If you email or reach out through social media, the representative or their staff will respond with their policy position. I've emailed my Republican senator many times about net neutrality (and other issues). While I've never felt like I was engaging in a true exchange of ideas, it does keep me in the loop on his voting record—and always renews my commitment to try and get someone else in office next election.

But it's not enough to learn the politics of the internet's infrastructure. We also have to *learn the politics of platforms.* Platforms love to create documents like "community guidelines," but these texts are usually hard to read, and companies can change them at will. Moreover, they're always top down rather than bottom up. Just like attending local zoning meetings can help new residents understand neighborhood tensions, learning the basics of web platform policies isn't hard, it just takes a little time. Platforms *can* change their policies if enough users make demands. As we learned in chapter 2, in 2014, Facebook changed its "real" name policy after queer, trans, and indigenous activists demanded new rules. To get there, users became activists. They learned platform policy in order to demand new rules. They built coalitions, organized protests, and made the platform meet their needs. In addition to organizing ourselves as users, we can support the efforts of tech workers who are pushing for change from within the industry. We can demand change from our platforms, but it means overcoming a sense of powerlessness, learning the stakes and stakeholders, and being thoughtful about how and with whom we spend our time online.

The steps I've outlined here aren't the only ways to push back against the isolation, displacement, and commercialization of a gentrified internet. They're just a way to get started in imagining a web that's different from what we have. There's a lot of cynicism and suspicion around Big Tech, and for good reason. But I want to end this book on a note of optimism—and a lesson from termites. In November 2019, I went to an event hosted by the Worker Solidarity Network in Philadelphia. The event brought together a group of activists to talk about their experiences fighting for racial equality and environmental justice. One of the activists, Janine Africa, spent nearly forty years in prison for her connection to MOVE, a radical political group based in Philadelphia. Asked about how to keep up a commitment to activist work, she responded with a metaphor about termites: "When termites start eating away at something, you don't see anything on the surface at first. It looks how it always has, smooth. But underneath, we're all just eating away. And over time, the whole structure comes down." Big Tech might seem like a force that can't be stopped. It has the support of capitalism, techno-optimists, and a whole lot of rich and powerful people. But if enough of us insist on carving out spaces that are inclusive and open, we just might be able to topple Big Tech and build something better.

List of Resources

Want to learn more about online and offline organizing but not sure where to start? Here is a *very* partial list of community groups, nonprofits, and think tanks that are working against urban gentrification and fighting for social justice with digital technology.

Antigentrification Organizations

Bronx Coalition for a Community Vision

A coalition of union members, tenants, residents, and faith leaders working toward affordable housing, good jobs and antidisplacement in the Bronx in New York City.

Color of Change

Color of Change is the largest online racial justice organization in the United States, combining projects on economic, criminal, media, and technological justice.

Empower DC

Since 2003, Empower DC has focused on racial, economic and environmental justice by building political power among the lowest income residents and communities of Washington, D.C.

Fifth Avenue Committee

Based in Brooklyn, New York, the Fifth Avenue Committee is devoted to advancing economic and social justice by demanding affordable housing, workforce development, and adult education programs.

LA Tenants Union

The LA Tenants Union builds neighborhood-based coalitions of renters and residents to demand rights for tenants, affordable housing, and an end to mass evictions.

National Coalition for Asian Pacific American Community Development

The National CAPACD is a coalition of roughly one hundred community organizations spanning twenty-one states and the Pacific Islands, with the goal of improving housing security and preserving Asian Pacific culture, particularly in low-income communities.

National Community Reinvestment Coalition

The NCRC uses grassroots organizing, policy, and advocacy work to promote access to basic banking, affordable housing, entrepreneurship, and job creation.

National Low Income Housing Coalition

Through policy work and research initiatives, NLIHC advocates for access to affordable housing for low-income people.

Next City

This nonprofit news organization supports research and reporting to support economic, environmental, and social justice in cities across the United States.

Nuestra Comunidad Development Corporation

NCDC is a community-driven group focused on the physical, economic, and social well-being of underserved populations in the Roxbury and Boston area of Massachusetts.

Philadelphia Tenants Union

Founded in 2016, the Philadelphia Tenants Union is a tenant-led organization committed to combatting eviction and promoting safe and affordable housing for renters in Philadelphia.

Right to the City Alliance

A national alliance of racial, economic, and environmental justice, RTTC works to combat gentrification and displacement of low-income people, POC, and LGBTQ folks.

Silicon Valley Rising

A community group committed to resisting gentrification, displacement, and homelessness in San Jose, California, by demanding family-supporting jobs, support for local schools, public transit, and community oversight.

South Bronx Unite

An all-volunteer coalition of South Bronx residents, community groups, and allies focused on protecting the social, environmental, and economic future of neighborhoods in the South Bronx in New York City.

Urban Displacement Project

A research and policy group based at UC Berkeley, UDP focuses on equitable development that can push back on gentrification and displacement.

Urban Reform Institute

Committed to sustainability and promoting economic inequality, the Urban Reform Institute advocates for a "people-oriented approach" to urban development, focusing on how planning and zoning can support communities instead of developers.

Women's Community Revitalization Project

The WCRP operates a community land trust in Philadelphia, Pennsylvania, promoting equitable real estate development through community ownership of property.

Tech and Social Justice Organizations

18 Million Rising

18MR brings Asian Americans together to build community through digital technology and popular culture.

AI Now

An interdisciplinary research center focused on the social implications of artificial intelligence technologies.

Black Girls Code

An organization committed to teaching coding to young Black women through educational programming, scholarships, and summer camps.

Carceral Tech Resistance Network

This network of technology activists facilitates trainings for radical community groups and builds tools, databases, and archives that document antiprivacy technologies.

Consentful Tech Project

A project that promotes user autonomy and online civil liberties by raising awareness and sharing skills to help ordinary people build and use digital tech.

Data & Society

Based in New York, Data & Society produces research and policy initiatives on artificial intelligence and automation, connections between work and health, and online disinformation.

Demand Progress

Demand Progress supports progressive policy changes through organizing and grassroots lobbying, focusing on digital civil liberties and government regulation of the tech industry.

Detroit Community Technology Project

DCTS trains neighborhood leaders in Detroit to support technological education and social justice organizing work.

Electronic Frontier Foundation

Since the 1990s, the EFF has advocated for user privacy, free speech online, and digital autonomy through litigation, policy advocacy, grassroots activism, and technology development.

Fight for the Future

A collective of artists, technologists, and activists coordinating online protests around net neutrality, countering surveillance, and promoting user privacy.

Free Press

Focused on media and technology, Free Press works toward equitable access to technology, diverse and independent media platforms, and community-based journalism.

MediaJustice

A grassroots initiative that supports communication rights, digital tech access, and community power.

National Hispanic Media Coalition

For over thirty years, the NHMC has advocated for greater representation of the Latinx community in print and digital media.

NYC Mesh

A collective of volunteers committed to ending the digital divide through building meshnets in New York City.

Open Technology Fund

OTF is a nonprofit organization promoting democratic values and fundamental human rights online.

Open Technology Institute

Focused on policy, OTI focuses on surveillance, consumer privacy, net neutrality, and broadband access.

Our Data Bodies

A research group committed to individual privacy, racial justice, and stopping government and corporate surveillance.

People's Open

A community owned and operated wireless tech group in Oakland, California, that builds mesh networks and offers skill-share programming.

Public Knowledge

Focusing on research and policy, Public Knowledge promotes free speech, an open internet, and access to digital tech.

Radical Reference

A collective of librarians, archivists, and information professionals committed to social justice and increasing access to technology.

Red Hook WiFi

Based in Brooklyn, New York, Red Hook WiFi is a community-led effort to close the digital divide using mesh networks and educational programming.

Resilient Just Technologies

A community technology project that promotes decentralized technologies for community groups committed to racial, economic, and climate justice.

Stop LAPD Spying Coalition

Based in Los Angeles and focused on the LAPD, this community group pushes back on police surveillance through collective action and advocacy.

Surveillance Technology Oversight Project

STOP is a nonprofit advocacy group and legal services provider committed to individual privacy and pushing back on state-level surveillance.

Tech Learning Collective

Based in New York City, the Tech Learning Collective is a technology school geared toward radical organizers, underserved communities, and organizations advancing social justice causes.

Tor Project

Most famous for creating a privacy-centric web browser, the Tor Project is a nonprofit committed to transparent digital tech and creating tools for activist groups.

TransTech

TransTech Provides networking and educational programming opportunities to LGBT people interested in digital technologies.

Tribal Digital Village

A project from the Southern California Tribal Chairmen's Association, the Tribal Digital Village provides internet access and promotes digital inclusion for tribal communities in Southern California.

Glossary

ANTITRUST A legal theory and form of legislation. The aim of antitrust legislation is to prevent or restrict monopolies, with the intention of promoting competition in business.

BBS An abbreviation for Bulletin Board System, a type of early computer network. BBSs are privately operated hubs for digital user groups, where users dial in to connect and share text files, code, and media. Although most BBSs either shut down or became ISPs in the late 1990s and early 2000s, a small number (about twenty) are still operating in North America.

BIG TECH Refers to major technology companies such as Apple, Google, Amazon, Microsoft, and Facebook. Big Tech includes these companies as well as smaller corporations that share the same goals, values, and priorities.

CALIFORNIA IDEOLOGY A term coined in the 1995 essay "The Californian Ideology," by English media theorists Richards Brook and Andy Cameron. The authors described the Californian Ideology as "dot.com liberalism," or a belief that technology is prosocial, and that the industry shouldn't be regulated by the state or federal government. See also *cyber-libertarianism*.

CYBER-LIBERTARIANISM A set of beliefs that sees technology as the means of promoting individual and social well-being. Like the California Ideology, cyber-libertarianism calls for decentralization, reduced dependence on central governments, and limited regulation.

FEDERAL COMMUNICATION COMMISSION (FCC) A government agency that regulates interstate and international communications throughout the United States, including in U.S. territories. The FCC is overseen by Congress and is responsible for implementing and enforcing U.S. communications law and regulations related to radio, television, phone, and internet.

FIDUCIARY RESPONSIBILITY A legal and financial term that describes a relationship where one party is required to act entirely on the other party's behalf and in their best interest. When a company sells stock to the public, it has a fiduciary responsibility to its shareholders to maximize shareholder profits.

FILTER BUBBLES A term used to describe online environments that act as echo chambers. In the context of digital life, filter bubbles are driven by algorithms that push similar content to users based on their past online behavior. Filter bubbles mean that people are exposed only to opinions and information that fit their existing beliefs. The term has been criticized for being too vague and panic-driven, and also for suggesting that echo chambers are newly created by digital tech rather than a longstanding part of ordinary social life.

FLIPPING HOUSES A profit-making strategy in real estate in which investors purchase a property at minimal cost and then make improvements to it in order to sell it at a higher price. For the most part, the term refers to companies and developers taking over properties rather than individual homeowners engaging in one-off improvement projects.

GENTRIFICATION At its most basic, *gentrification* refers to a process of neighborhood change. Gentrification involves a transition of people and resources, where upper- and middle-class people move into neighborhoods previously inhabited by less affluent residents. The result is typically the displacement of original residents, increasingly homogenous culture, and uneven commercialization of businesses.

INITIAL PUBLIC OFFERING (IPO) A stock market launch or the initial sale of a company's stock to the public. Through this process, also known as *floating* or *going public*, a privately held company becomes a public company.

INTERNET RELAY CHAT (IRC) A chat protocol developed for internet-based communication. In an IRC, clients connect to a specified server that is part of a collection of servers known as an IRC network. If a client sends a message to a user on a different server within the same IRC network, the message is relayed between the servers and then to the other client. Like BBSs, IRCs have faded in popularity, but some are still in operation.

INTERNET SERVICE PROVIDER (ISP) An organization that provides services for accessing the Internet. ISPs can be commercial, community-owned, nonprofit, or privately owned. Services typically provided by ISPs include internet access, internet transit, domain name registration, and web hosting.

INVESTMENT PROPERTY A real estate property purchased with the intent of earning a return on the initial investment either through rental income, the future resale of the property due to increased value, or both.

IRL An abbreviation for "in real life." Often used in online communication to let people you are talking about something happening in a face-to-face context rather than something happening only online.

LAST MILE PROBLEM The *last mile problem* has to do with the labor and materials needed to connect people and communication infrastructure, such as the cables needed for telephone and internet access. The distance between the network hub and the residential or commercial access points, typically the last 20 percent of the overall network, is referred to as the "last mile." This 20 percent can account for 80 percent of the costs for the entire network.

MERITOCRACY A value system where economic goods and/or political power are meant to be given to individuals based on talent, effort, and achievement rather than wealth or social class. The idea behind meritocracy is to ignore *who someone is* and evaluate people only on *what they do.* But meritocracy often imagines a level playing field and doesn't consider how power and privilege shape opportunities and performance.

MESH NETWORKS A type of wireless network where the connection is spread out among many wireless mesh nodes that connect with one another to share the network connection across a much larger area, as opposed to traditional networks, which rely on a small number of wired access points controlled by ISPs. Also called meshnets, mesh networks can be operated by community groups, nonprofits, or commercial providers.

NET NEUTRALITY Both a political movement and a policy proposal, net neutrality argues that internet service providers and broadband network providers should be completely neutral about the content sent over their networks. Net neutrality activists believe in strong federal regulation to ensure that providers treat all internet traffic equally, regardless of its content, source, or destination.

PLATFORM Strictly defined, a piece of software that makes it possible to scrape data through an application programming interface (API). However, the term can also be used more generally to refer to websites that allow users to create content. Facebook, Twitter, and Instagram are all examples of social media platforms.

REDLINING The systematic denial of various services based on race, class, or other identity markers. Redlining can happen directly, by refusing to provide services to individual people, or indirectly, through the selective raising of prices for potential buyers. In the United States, well-known examples of redlining have involved the denial of services like banking, insurance, and real estate to people of color.

TAX ABATEMENT The reduction of or exemption from taxes granted by a government for a specified period, usually to encourage activities like investment in property. (Tax incentives are a form of tax abatement.) Tax abatements can lure developers into a neighborhood with affordable housing, ultimately raising average property values and property tax rates.

TECHNO-DETERMINIST Someone who assumes that technology is the main driver for social change. In other words, techno-determinists assume technological causes are at work when social processes shift or change.

TECHNO-SKEPTICISM Instead of seeing technology as a positive force for social change, techno-skeptics are cynical or suspicious of the benefits of modern technology in society.

Sources and Further Reading

It's impossible to write a book without relying on research, data, and viewpoints from other people. At the same time, academic conventions of citation can feel overwhelming or tedious to a general audience. As a compromise between accessibility and acknowledging source material, I have worked to provide enough information in the text for readers to find sources in the bibliography. Listed below, in alphabetical order by chapter, are the sources that I drew on. My goal in presenting sources in this way is to acknowledge the texts that made it possible to write this book and also to give interested readers some additional sources on the topics of each chapter. In chapter 2, in addition to the articles, blog posts, and books that I used as sources, I reference a small number of interviews that were conducted in my previous research on countercultural communities online.

Chapter 1

Arthur, G. 2015. "Lack of Internet Access Makes Climb Out of Poverty Harder." *Al Jazeera*, October 24, 2015. http://america.aljazeera.com/articles/2015/10/24/not-having-internet-access-at-home-hinders-education-employment.html.

Baker, K. 2018. "The Death of a Once Great City." *Harper's Magazine,* July 2018. https://harpers.org/archive/2018/07/the-death-of-new-york-city-gentrification.

Beckett, L., D. BondGraham, P. Andringa, and A. Clayton. 2019. "Gun Violence Has Sharply Declined in California's Bay Area. What Happened?" *Guardian,* June 4, 2019. www.theguardian.com/us-news/ng-interactive/2019/jun/03/gun-violence-bay-area-drop-30-percent-why-investigation.

Beswick, J., G. Alexandri, M. Byrne, S. Vives-Miró, D. Fields, S. Hodkinson, and M. Janoschka. 2016. "Speculating on London's Housing Future: The Rise of Global Corporate Landlords in 'Post-Crisis' Urban Landscapes." *City* 20 (2): 321–41.

Brown-Saracino, J., ed. 2013. *The Gentrification Debates: A Reader.* New York: Routledge.

———. 2013. "Social Preservationists and the Quest for Authentic Community." In *The Gentrification Debates: A Reader,* edited by J. Brown-Saracino, 261–75. New York: Routledge.

Bruns, A. 2019. "It's Not the Technology, Stupid: How the 'Echo Chamber' and 'Filter Bubble' Metaphors Have Failed Us." Paper presented at the International Association for Media and Communication Research, Madrid, Spain, July 7–11, 2019. https://eprints.qut.edu.au/131675/1/It%E2%80%99s%20Not%20the%20Technology%2C%20Stupid%20%28paper%2019771%29.pdf.

Butler, T. 2013. "Consumption and Culture." In *The Gentrification Debates: A Reader,* edited by J. Brown-Saracino, 235–60. New York: Routledge.

Chun, W. H. K. 2018. "Queerying Homophily." *Mediarep.* https://mediarep.org/bitstream/handle/doc/13259/Pattern_Discrimination_59–97_Chun_Queerying_Homophily.pdf?sequence=1.

Coates, T. 2014. "The Case for Reparations." *Atlantic,* June 2014. www.theatlantic.com/magazine/archive/2014/06/the-case-for-reparations/361631.

Department of Housing and Urban Development. 2015. "HUD & Associated Bank Reach Historic $200 Million Settlement of 'Redlining' Claim." https://archives.hud.gov/news/2015/pr15-064b.cfm.

Ernsthausen, J., E. Simani, and A. Shaw. 2020. "Can You Be Evicted during Coronavirus? Here's How to Find Out." *ProPublica,* May 18, 2020. www

.propublica.org/article/can-you-be-evicted-during-coronavirus-heres-how-to-find-out.

Fields, D., A. Schafran, and Z. Taylor. 2017. "Wall Street Landlords Are Chasing the American Dream—Here's What It Means for Families." *Conversation,* September 7, 2017. https://theconversation.com/wall-street-landlords-are-chasing-the-american-dream-heres-what-it-means-for-families-82146.

Fields, D., and S. Uffer. 2016. "The Financialisation of Rental Housing: A Comparative Analysis of New York City and Berlin." *Urban Studies* 53 (7): 1486–502.

Gibbs, S. 2016. "Mobile Web Browsing Overtakes Desktop for the First Time." *Guardian,* November 2, 2016. www.theguardian.com/technology /2016/nov/02/mobile-web-browsing-desktop-smartphones-tablets.

Goldstone, B. 2019. "The New American Homeless." *New Republic,* August 21, 2019. https://newrepublic.com/article/154618/new-american-homeless-housing-insecurity-richest-cities.

Halegoua, G. R. 2019. *The Digital City: Media and the Social Production of Place.* New York: NYU Press.

Jamieson, K. H. 2018. *Cyberwar: How Russian Hackers and Trolls Helped Elect a President; What We Don't, Can't, and Do Know.* Oxford: Oxford University Press.

Lane, B. 2019. "Blackstone Sells Off More than $1 Billion in Shares of Invitation Homes." *HousingWire,* May 30, 2019. www.housingwire.com /articles/49216-blackstone-sells-off-more-than-1-billion-in-shares-of-invitation-homes.

Lindeman, T. 2019. "Nearly 40 Percent of Toronto Condos Not Owner-Occupied, New Figures Reveal." *Guardian,* July 7, 2019. www.theguardian .com/world/2019/jul/07/toronto-housing-owner-occupied-canada-affordability.

McChesney, R. W. 2013. *Digital Disconnect: How Capitalism Is Turning the Internet against Democracy.* New York: New Press.

McKenney, K. 2016. "The UN Declares the Internet a Basic Human Right." *Paste Magazine,* July 5, 2016. www.pastemagazine.com/articles /2016/07/the-un-declares-internet-access-a-basic-human-righ .html.

Menegus, B. 2019. "Mark Zuckerberg Is a Slumlord." *Gizmodo,* August 20, 2019. https://gizmodo.com/mark-zuckerberg-is-a-slumlord-1837375095.

Newman, K. 2019. "San Francisco Is Home to the Highest Density of Billionaires." *U.S. News,* May 10, 2019. www.usnews.com/news/cities /articles/2019-05-10/san-francisco-is-home-to-the-worlds-most-billion-aires-per-capita.

Pariser, E. 2011. *The Filter Bubble: What the Internet Is Hiding from You.* London: Penguin UK.

Perez, G. M. 2002. "The Other 'Real World': Gentrification and the Social Construction of Place in Chicago." *Urban Anthropology and Studies of Cultural Systems and World Economic Development* 31 (1): 37–68.

Polonski, V. 2016. "Is Social Media Destroying Democracy?" *Newsweek,* August 5, 2016. www.newsweek.com/social-media-destroying-democracy-487483.

Raymond, E., R. Duckworth, B. Miller, M. Lucas, and S. Pokharel. 2016. "Corporate Landlords, Institutional Investors, and Displacement: Eviction Rates in Single Family Renters." Federal Reserve Bank of Atlanta, Community and Economic Development Discussion Paper No. 04-16, December 2016. www.frbatlanta.org/-/media/documents/community-development/publications/discussion-papers/2016/04-corporate-land-lords-institutional-investors-and-displacement-2016-12-21.pdf.

Rose, D. 2013. "Rethinking Gentrification: Beyond the Uneven Development of Marxist Urban Theory." In *The Gentrification Debates: A Reader,* edited by J. Brown-Saracino, 195–210. New York: Routledge.

Rosenthal, T. J. 2019. "101 Notes on the LA Tenants Union." *Commune,* July 19, 2019. https://communemag.com/101-notes-on-the-la-tenants-union.

Smith, N. 1996. *The New Urban Frontier.* London: Routledge.

———. 2013. "Building the Frontier Myth." In *The Gentrification Debates: A Reader,* edited by J. Brown-Saracino, 113–17. New York: Routledge.

Statista. 2020. "Worldwide Market Share of Search Engines from January 2010 to July 2020." August 2020. www.statista.com/statistics/216573 /worldwide-market-share-of-search-engines.

United Nations. 2014. "World's Population Increasingly Urban with More than Half Living in Urban Areas." July 10, 2014. www.un.org/en/development /desa/news/population/world-urbanization-prospects-2014.html.

Vaidhyanathan, S. 2018. *Antisocial Media: How Facebook Disconnects Us and Undermines Democracy*. Oxford: Oxford University Press.

Zukin, S. 2013. "Gentrification as Market and Place." In *The Gentrification Debates: A Reader,* edited by J. Brown-Saracino, 37–44. New York: Routledge.

Chapter 2

Angwin, J., and T. Parris. 2016. "Facebook Lets Advertisers Exclude Users by Race." *ProPublica,* October 28, 2016. www.propublica.org/article /facebook-lets-advertisers-exclude-users-by-race.

Body Modification E-Zine. n.d. BME (website). Accessed May 26, 2020. www.bme.com.

Bossewitch, J., and A. Sinnreich. 2013. "The End of Forgetting: Strategic Agency beyond the Panopticon." *New Media & Society* 15 (2): 224–42.

boyd, d. 2013. "White Flight in Networked Publics: How Race and Class Shaped American Teen Engagement with MySpace and Facebook." In *Race after the Internet,* edited by L. Nakamura and P. A. Chow-White, 203–22. New York: Routledge.

Brock, A., Jr. 2020. *Distributed Blackness: African American Cybercultures*. New York: NYU Press.

Brunton, F. 2013. *Spam: A Shadow History of the Internet*. Cambridge, MA: MIT Press.

Brunton, F., and H. Nissenbaum. 2015. *Obfuscation: A User's Guide for Privacy and Protest*. Cambridge, MA: MIT Press.

Clark-Parsons, R., and J. Lingel. 2020. "Margins as Methods, Margins as Ethics: A Feminist Framework for Studying Online Alterity." *Social Media + Society* 6 (1). https://doi.org/10.1177/2056305120913994.

Clement, J. 2019. "Tumblr—Statistics & Facts." Statista, August 20, 2019. www.statista.com/topics/2463/tumblr.

Department of Housing and Urban Development. 2019. "HUD Charges Facebook with Housing Discrimination over Company's Targeted Advertising Process." March 28, 2019. www.hud.gov/press/press_ releases_media_advisories/HUD_No_19_035.

Elgakhlab, F. 2019. "Vox Sentences: Facebook's Digital Redlining." *Vox,* March 28, 2019. www.vox.com/vox-sentences/2019/3/28/18286216 /Facebook-digital-redlining-israel-un-golan-heights.

Eubanks, V. 2012. *Digital Dead End: Fighting for Social Justice in the Informa-tion Age.* Cambridge, MA: MIT Press.

———. 2018. *Automating Inequality: How High-Tech Tools Profile, Police, and Punish the Poor.* New York: St. Martin's Press.

Karppi, T. 2019. *Disconnect: Facebook's Affective Bonds.* Minneapolis: Univer-sity of Minnesota Press.

Kennedy, H. 2006. "Beyond Anonymity, or Future Directions for Internet Identity Research." *New Media and Society* 8 (6): 859–76.

Lesbianrey. 2019. "mandatory disclosure that i do think this site sucks but. . . . . .tumblr's kinda nice in that its less like. . .. . .public facing than twitter fb insta etc?" Tumblr, August 28, 2019. https://susieboboozy .tumblr.com/post/187336230363/guardiankarenterrier-amourboi-lynati.

Lewis, T., S. P. Gangadharan, M. Saba, and T. Petty. 2018. *Digital Defense Playbook: Community Power Tools for Reclaiming Data.* Detroit: Our Data Bodies.

Lingel, J. 2012. "Ethics and Dilemmas of Online Ethnography." In *CHI'12 Extended Abstracts on Human Factors in Computing Systems,* edited by J. A. Konstan, 41–50. New York: Association for Computing Machinery.

———. 2017. *Digital Countercultures and the Struggle for Community.* Cam-bridge, MA: MIT Press.

———. 2020. *An Internet for the People: The Politics and Promise of Craigslist.* Princeton, NJ: Princeton University Press.

Lingel, J., A. Trammell, J. Sanchez, and M. Naaman. 2012. "Practices of Information and Secrecy in a Punk Rock Subculture." In *Proceedings of the ACM 2012 Conference on Computer Supported Cooperative Work,* edited by S. Poltrock and C. Simone, 157–66. New York: Association for Computing Machinery.

Maciag, M. 2015. "Oakland Gentrification Maps and Data." Governing: The Future of States and Localities, February 1, 2015. www.governing.com /gov-data/oakland-gentrification-maps-demographic-data.html.

Noble, S. U. 2018. *Algorithms of Oppression: How Search Engines Reinforce Racism.* New York: NYU Press.

Pariser, E. 2011. *The Filter Bubble: What the Internet Is Hiding from You.* London: Penguin UK.

Petrusich, A. 2016. "The Music Critic in the Age of the Insta-release." *New Yorker,* March 9, 2016. www.newyorker.com/culture/cultural-comment/the-music-critic-in-the-age-of-the-insta-release.

Renninger, B. J. 2015. "'Where I Can Be Myself . . . Where I Can Speak My Mind': Networked Counterpublics in a Polymedia Environment." *New Media & Society* 17 (9): 1513–29.

Romano, A. 2018. "Tumblr Is Banning Adult Content. It's about So Much More than Porn." *Vox,* December 4, 2018. www.vox.com/2018/12/4/18124120/tumblr-porn-adult-content-ban-user-backlash.

Snakegay. 2019. "everyone who buys tumblr fundamentally misunderstands the fact that us clowns that still use this site use it specifically because its a no mans land in here." Tumblr, August 30, 2019. https://susieboboozy.tumblr.com/post/187371664168/snakegay-everyone-who-buys-tumblr-fundamentally.

Tiidenberg, K. 2016. "Boundaries and Conflict in a NSFW Community on Tumblr: The Meanings and Uses of Selfies." *New Media & Society* 18 (8): 1563–78.

Tufekci, Z. 2018. "Yes, Big Platforms Could Change Their Business Models." *Wired,* December 17, 2018. www.wired.com/story/big-platforms-could-change-business-models.

U.S. Government Accountability Office. 2016. "K-12 Education: Better Use of Information Could Help Agency Identify Disparities and Address Racial Discrimination." April 21, 2016. www.gao.gov/products/GAO-16-345.

Wheaton, W. 2018. "I just want to belabor this point for a moment. These images are not explicit. These pictures show two adults, engaging in consensual kissing. That's it." Tumblr, December 3, 2018. https://wilwheaton.tumblr.com/post/180770332474/i-just-want-to-belabor-this-point-for-a-moment.

Chapter 3

Abbate, J. 2000. *Inventing the Internet.* Cambridge, MA: MIT Press.

———. 2012. *Recoding Gender: Women's Changing Participation in Computing.* Cambridge, MA: MIT Press.

Ames, M. 2019. *The Charisma Machine: The Life, Death, and Legacy of One Laptop per Child*. Cambridge, MA: MIT Press.

Ankerson, M. S. 2010. "Web Industries, Economies, Aesthetics: Mapping the Look of the Web in the Dot-Com Era." In *Web History*, edited by N. Brügger, 173–93. New York: Peter Lang.

———. 2012. "Writing Web Histories with an Eye on the Analog Past." *New Media and Society* 14 (3): 384–400.

———. 2018. *Dot-Com Design: The Rise of a Usable, Social, Commercial Web*. New York: NYU Press.

Aupperlee, A. 2018. "Duolingo CEO Has Message for 'Idiots' Mad about Hiring Equal Number of Women." *TribLive*, February 14, 2018. https://archive.triblive.com/business/technology/duolingo-ceo-has-message-for-idiots-mad-about-hiring-equal-number-of-women.

Baker, J. 2019. *The Antitrust Paradigm: Restoring a Competitive Economy*. Cambridge, MA: Harvard University Press.

Banet-Weiser, S. 2018. *Empowered: Popular Feminism and Popular Misogyny*. Durham, NC: Duke University Press.

Brigham, K. 2019. "How Amazon Makes Money." *CNBC*, February 13. www.cnbc.com/2019/02/12/how-amazon-makes-money.html.

Brinklow, A. 2017. "SF Tech Company Offers Employees $10K to Move outside Bay Area." *SF Curbed*, March 20, 2017. https://sf.curbed.com/2017/3/20/14986354/zapier-delocation-move-away-san-francisco.

Buckmaster, J. 2010. "An Open Invitation to Rachel Lloyd." *Craigslist Blog*, May 11, 2010. http://blog.craigslist.org/2010/05/11/an-open-invitation-to-rachel-lloyd.

Chandra, V. 2014. "What India Can Teach Silicon Valley about Its Gender Problem." *Wired*, August 28, 2014. www.wired.com/2014/08/silicon-valley-sexism.

Chang, E. 2019. *Brotopia: Breaking Up the Boys' Club of Silicon Valley*. New York: Portfolio.

Chavez, Y. 2019. "An Open Letter to Google CEO Sundar Pichai." *Medium*, June 18, 2019. https://medium.com/@yolanda.chavez.sanjose/an-open-letter-to-google-ceo-sundar-pichai-baa1c8f155f3.

Curtis, S. 2015. "Is Facebook Becoming the Internet?" *Telegraph*, February 10, 2015. www.telegraph.co.uk/technology/Facebook/11402343/Is-Facebook-becoming-the-internet.html.

Davis, A. 2019. "Why Amazon Paid No 2018 US Federal Income tax." *CNBC,*
April 4, 2019. www.cnbc.com/2019/04/03/why-amazon-paid-no-federal-
income-tax.html

De Nisco Rayome, N. 2018. "Eye Opening Statistics about Minorities in
Tech." *Techrepublic,* February 7, 2018. www.techrepublic.com/article/5-
eye-opening-statistics-about-minorities-in-tech.

D'Ignazio, C., and L. F Klein. 2020. *Data Feminism.* Cambridge, MA: MIT Press.

Fattal, A. 2012. "Facebook: Corporate Hackers, a Billion Users, and the
Geo-Politics of the "Social Graph.'" *Anthropological Quarterly* 85 (3):
927–55.

Finley, K. 2013. "New Study Exposes Gender Bias in Tech Job Listings."
Wired, March 11, 2013. www.wired.com/2013/03/hiring-women.

Florida, R. 2019. "6 Rules for Better, More Inclusive Economic Development
in Cities." *CityLab,* February 26, 2019. www.citylab.com/perspective/2019
/02/amazon-hq2-new-york-incentives-economic-development-cities
/583540.

Galbraith, R. 2015. "The Tech Industry Is Stripping San Francisco of Its
Culture, and Your City Could Be Next." *Newsweek,* October 1, 2015. www
.newsweek.com/san-francisco-tech-industry-gentrification-documentary-
378628.

Galvin, G. 2016. "Study: Middle School Is Key to Girls' Coding Interest." *U.S.
News,* October 20, 2016. www.usnews.com/news/data-mine/articles/2016-
10-20/study-computer-science-gender-gap-widens-despite-increase-
in-jobs.

Glaser, A. 2020. "Current and Ex-Employees Allege Google Drastically
Rolled Back Diversity and Inclusion Programs." *NBC News,* May 13, 2020.
www.nbcnews.com/news/us-news/current-ex-employees-allege-google-
drastically-rolled-back-diversity-inclusion-n1206181.

———. 2020. "House Democrats Press Google over Report of Scaled Back
Diversity Efforts." *CNBC,* May 18, 2020. www.cnbc.com/2020/05/18
/house-democrats-press-google-over-report-of-scaled-back-diversity-
efforts.html.

Glazer, A. 2019. "Everything You Think You Know about Corporate Tax
Incentives Is Wrong." *Fast Company,* February 25, 2019. www.fastcompany
.com/90310500/everything-you-think-you-know-about-corporate-tax-
incentives-is-wrong.

Griffith, E. 2017. "The Other Tech Bubble." *Wired,* December 16, 2017. www
.wired.com/story/the-other-tech-bubble.

Hern, A. 2019. "Google Pays 11 Million to Jobseekers Who Allege Age Discrimination." *Guardian,* July 22, 2019. www.theguardian.com/technology/2019
/jul/22/google-pays-11m-to-jobseekers-who-alleged-age-discrimination.

Hess, A. 2020. "Coronavirus Highlights the Inequality of Who Can—and
Can't—Work from Home." *CNBC,* March 4, 2020. www.cnbc.com/2020/03
/04/coronavirus-highlights-who-can-and-cant-work-from-home.html.

Ho, V. 2019. "Google to Invest $1bn to Fight Tech-Fueled Housing Crisis."
Guardian, June 18, 2019. www.theguardian.com/technology/2019/jun/18
/google-housing-homelessness-tech-industry-investment.

Holder, S. 2019. "Dueling GoFundMe Campaigns Highlight a San Francisco
NIMBY Battle." *CityLab,* April 3, 2019. www.citylab.com/equity/2019/04
/san-francisco-homeless-shelter-embarcadero-gofundme-nimby
/586252.

Hollister, S. 2019. "Google Pledges $1 Billion." *Verge,* June 18, 2019. www
.theverge.com/2019/6/18/18683827/google-silicon-valley-housing-crisis-
1-billion-investment-sf-bay-area.

Hong, R. 2016. "Soft Skills and Hard Numbers: Gender Discourse in
Human Resources." *Big Data & Society* 3 (2). https://doi.org/10.1177
/2053951716674237.

Johnson, S. 2018. "The Political Education of Silicon Valley." *Wired* 26 (8): 64–73.

Kapor Center. 2017. "Tech Leavers Study." https://mkokaporcenter5ld71a
.kinstacdn.com/wp-content/uploads/2017/08/TechLeavers2017.pdf.

Kelly, J. 2020. "After Announcing Twitter's Permanent Remote-Work Policy,
Jack Dorsey Extends Same Courtesy to Square Employees." *Forbes,* May
19, 2020. www.forbes.com/sites/jackkelly/2020/05/19/after-announcing-
twitters-permanent-work-from-home-policy-jack-dorsey-extends-same-
courtesy-to-square-employees-this-could-change-the-way-people-work-
where-they-live-and-how-much-theyll-be-paid/#549bc56e614b.

Kendall, M. 2017. "How Silicon Valley Silences Sexual Harassment Victims."
San Jose Mercury News, July 16, 2017. www.mercurynews.com/2017/07/16
/how-silicon-valley-silences-sexual-harassment-victims.

Khan, L. M. 2016. "Amazon's Antitrust Paradox." *Yale Law Journal* 126 (3):
710–805.

Koran, M. 2019. "Black Facebook Staff Describe Workplace Racism in Anonymous Letter." *Guardian,* November 13, 2019. www.theguardian .com/technology/2019/nov/13/facebook-discrimination-black-workers-letter.

Kosoff, M. 2017. "Silicon Valley's Sexual Harassment Crisis Keeps Getting Worse." *Vanity Fair,* September 12, 2017. www.vanityfair.com/news/2017 /09/silicon-valleys-sexual-harassment-crisis-keeps-getting-worse.

Kulwin, N. 2018. "We Can Solve Huge Technical Issues, but Can't Pay Our Employees a Fair Wage?" *New York Magazine,* April 16, 2018. https:// nymag.com/intelligencer/2018/04/ellen-pao-reddit-ceo-interview .html.

Lafrance, A. 2016. "Is Silicon Valley a Meritocracy?" *Atlantic,* October 13, 2016. www.theatlantic.com/technology/archive/2016/10/is-silicon-valley-a-meritocracy/503948.

Luckie, M. 2018. "Facebook Is Failing Its Black Employees and Its Black Users." Facebook, November 27, 2018. www.facebook.com/notes/mark-s-luckie/facebook-is-failing-its-black-employees-and-its-black-users /1931075116975013.

Marwick, A. E. 2013. *Status Update: Celebrity, Publicity, and Branding in the Social Media Age.* New Haven, CT: Yale University Press.

Meyer, R. 2018. "How to Fight Amazon (before You Turn 29)." *Atlantic,* August 15, 2018. www.theatlantic.com/magazine/archive/2018/07/lina-khan-antitrust/561743.

Meyersohn, N. 2018. "After the Crisis, Silicon Valley Overtook Wall Street as the Place to Be." *CNN,* June 7, 2018. https://money.cnn.com/2018/06/07 /news/economy/wall-street-silicon-valley-google-goldman-sachs/index .html.

Miller, M. 2016. "'Tech Bro' Calls San Francisco 'Shanty Town,' Decries Homeless 'Riffraff' in Open Letter." *Chicago Tribune,* February 18, 2016. www.chicagotribune.com/business/blue-sky/ct-tech-bro-letter-san-francisco-homeless-20160218-story.html.

Nedzhvetskaya, N., and J.S. Tan. 2019. "What We Learned from Over a Decade of Tech Activism." *Guardian,* December 22, 2019. www.theguardian.com /commentisfree/2019/dec/22/tech-worker-activism-2019-what-we-learned.

Paul, K. 2019. "Google Rejects Plans to Fight Sexual Harassment and Boost Diversity." *Guardian,* June 19, 2019. www.theguardian.com/technology /2019/jun/19/google-alphabet-shareholder-meeting-protest-sexual-harassment.

Policy Link. n.d. "Oakland's Displacement Crisis: As Told by the Numbers." Accessed May 25, 2020. www.policylink.org/sites/default/files/PolicyLink %20Oakland%27s%20Displacement%20Crisis%20by%20the%20 numbers.pdf.

Shapiro, C. 2019. "Protecting Competition in the American Economy: Merger Control, Tech Titans, Labor Markets." *Journal of Economic Perspectives* 33(3): 69–93.

ShowTech. 2017. "The Gender Gap in the Tech Industry." https://showtech .io/blog/10-08-2020-the-gender-gap-in-the-tech-industry.

Smith, N. 1996. *The New Urban Frontier.* London: Routledge.

Solon, O. 2017. "Ashamed to Work in Silicon Valley: How Techies Became the New Bankers." *Guardian,* November 8, 2017. www.theguardian.com /technology/2017/nov/08/ashamed-to-work-in-silicon-valley-how-techies-became-the-new-bankers.

Szmigiera, M. 2020. "Number of Merger and Acquisition Transactions Worldwide from 1985 to 2019." Statista, February 24, 2020. www.statista .com/statistics/267368/number-of-mergers-and-acquisitions-worldwide-since-2005.

Turner, F. 2009. "Burning Man at Google: A Cultural Infrastructure for New Media Production." *New Media & Society* 11 (1–2): 73–94.

———. 2010. *From Counterculture to Cyberculture: Stewart Brand, the Whole Earth Network, and the Rise of Digital Utopianism.* Chicago: University of Chicago Press.

U.S. Equal Employment Opportunity Commission. 2016. "Diversity in High Tech." www.eeoc.gov/special-report/diversity-high-tech.

Warschauer, M., and M. Ames. 2010. "Can One Laptop per Child Save the World's Poor?" *Journal of International Affairs* 46 (1): 33–51.

Wiener, A. 2016. "Why Can't Silicon Valley Cover Its Diversity Problem?" *New Yorker,* November 26, 2016. www.newyorker.com/business/currency /why-cant-silicon-valley-solve-its-diversity-problem.

Wu, T. 2018. *The Curse of Bigness: Antitrust in the New Gilded Age.* New York: Columbia Global Reports.

Chapter 4

Abbate, J. 2000. *Inventing the Internet*. Cambridge, MA: MIT Press.

Ankerson, M. S. 2018. *Dot-Com Design: The Rise of a Usable, Social, Commercial Web*. New York: NYU Press.

Berner, A.-S. 2018. "Red Hook: The Hip New York Enclave Caught between Gentrification and Climate Change." *Guardian,* September 25, 2018. www .theguardian.com/environment/2018/sep/25/red-hook-climate-change-floodplain-hurricane-sandy-gentrification.

Bettilyon, T. E. 2017. "Network Neutrality: A History of Common Carrier Laws 1884–2018." *Medium,* December 12, 2017. https://medium.com/@ TebbaVonMathenstien/network-neutrality-a-history-of-common-carrier-laws-1884-2018-2b592f22ed2e.

Bowker, G. C., and S. L. Star. 2000. *Sorting Things Out: Classification and Its Consequences*. Cambridge, MA: MIT Press.

Center for Digital Democracy. 2016. "Big Data Is Watching: Growing Data Digital Surveillance of Consumers by ISPs and Other Leading Video Providers." www.democraticmedia.org/sites/default/files/field/public-files/2016/ispbigdatamarch2016.pdf.

Driscoll, K. E. 2014. "Hobbyist Inter-networking and the Popular Internet Imaginary: Forgotten Histories of Networked Personal Computing, 1978–1998." PhD diss., University of Southern California.

Dunbar-Hester, C. 2014. *Low Power to the People: Pirates, Protest, and Politics in FM Radio Activism*. MIT Press: Cambridge, MA.

Edwards, B. 2016. "The Lost Civilization of Dial-Up Bulletin Board Systems." *Atlantic,* November 4, 2016. www.theatlantic.com/technology/archive /2016/11/the-lost-civilization-of-dial-up-bulletin-board-systems/506465.

Federal Communication Commission. 2011. "Nonprofit Media." https:// transition.fcc.gov/osp/inc-report/INoC-31-Nonprofit-Media.pdf.

———. 2015. "Eighth Broadband Progress Report." August 23, 2015. www.fcc .gov/reports-research/reports/broadband-progress-reports/eighth-broad-band-progress-report.

Finley, K. 2018. "The WIRED Guide to Net Neutrality." *Wired,* September 5, 2018. www.wired.com/story/guide-net-neutrality.

Greenstein, S. 2015. *How the Internet Became Commercial: Innovation, Privatization, and the Birth of a New Network*. Princeton, NJ: Princeton University Press.

Haleguoa, G. 2016. "'Always Off' Connection." *Flow*, October 24, 2016. www .flowjournal.org/2016/10/always-off-connection.

Haleguoa, G. R., and J. Lingel. 2018. "Lit Up and Left Dark: Failures of Imagination in Urban Broadband Networks." *New Media & Society* 20 (12): 4634–52.

Hu, T. H. 2015. *A Prehistory of the Cloud*. Cambridge, MA: MIT Press.

Kensinger, N. 2016. "Red Hook's Long, Inevitable Gentrification Divides Community." *Curbed*, January 28, 2016. https://ny.curbed.com/2016/1/28 /10872092/red-hooks-long-inevitable-gentrification-divides-community.

Lewis, T., S. P. Gangadharan, M. Saba, and T. Petty. 2018. *Digital Defense Playbook: Community Power Tools for Reclaiming Data*. Detroit: Our Data Bodies.

Lotman, M. 2018. "The Disclaimer." *Technoskeptic* 1 (1): 1–5.

Meinrath, S., and V. Pickard. 2008. "Transcending Net Neutrality: Ten Steps toward an Open Internet." *Education Week Commentary* 12 (6): 1–12.

Muíneacháin, C. 2012. "Thanks, Al Gore [Podcast #30]." *Technology*, May 24, 2012. http://technology.ie/thanks-al-gore-podcast-30.

National Science Foundation. 2003. "A Brief History of the NSF and the Internet." August 13, 2003. www.nsf.gov/news/news_summ.jsp?cntn_id= 103050.

Newnham, N., and J. LeBrecht, directors. 2020. *Crip Camp: A Disability Revolution*. Documentary film. Chicago: Higher Ground Productions.

People's Open. 2020. "Frequently Asked Questions." https://peoplesopen .net/learn/faqs.

Pickard, V., and D. Berman. 2019. *After Net Neutrality: A New Deal for the Digital Age*. New Haven, CT: Yale University Press.

Quail, C., and C. Larabie. 2010. "Net Neutrality: Media Discourses and Public Perception." *Global Media Journal* 3 (1): 31–50.

Red Hook Wifi. 2020. Red Hook Wifi (website). https://redhookwifi.org.

Sandvig, C. 2007. "Network Neutrality Is the New Common Carriage." *Info: The Journal of Policy, Regulation and Strategy for Telecommunications, Information and Media* 9 (2–3): 136–47.

Schuster, J. 2016. "A Brief History of Internet Service Providers." *Exede*. https://web.archive.org/web/20190428045452/https://www.exede.com /blog/brief-history-internet-service-providers.

Shaffer, D. 2018. "Who Controls the Internet? A State-by-State Look." *WebFX,* December 21, 2018. www.webfx.com/blog/internet/who-controls-the-internet-a-state-by-state-look.

Silverman, G. 2013. "Do-It-Yourself Internet in Brooklyn." *Washington Post,* October 4, 2013. www.washingtonpost.com/video/video/thefold/do-it-yourself-internet-in-brooklyn/2013/10/04/796abb5c-2ba8-11e3-b139-029811dbb57f_video.html?noredirect=on&utm_term=.52bfdc0c01da.

Sinnreich, A., N. Graham, and A. Trammell. 2011. "Weaving a New 'Net': A Mesh-Based Solution for Democratizing Networked Communications." *Information Society* 27 (5): 336–45.

Skycoin. 2018. "Net Neutrality and the Tyranny of the ISPs." *Medium,* November 11, 2018. https://medium.com/skycoin/net-neutrality-and-the-tyranny-of-the-isps-3f2414f91fce.

Smith, J. 2016. "This DIY Innovation Is Helping Activists Take Back the Internet from Time Warner Cable." *Mic,* January 28, 2016. www.mic.com/articles/133665/this-diy-innovation-is-helping-activists-take-back-the-internet-from-time-warner-cable.

Starosielski, N. 2015. *The Undersea Network.* Durham, NC: Duke University Press.

Wu, T. 2003. "Network Neutrality, Broadband Discrimination." *Journal of Telecommunications and High Technology Law* 2, 141.

Wu, T., and C. S. Yoo. 2007. "Keeping the Internet Neutral? Tim Wu and Christopher Yoo Debate." *Federal Communications Law Journal* 53 (9). www.repository.law.indiana.edu/fclj/vol59/iss3/6/.

Yoo, C. 2018. "Common Carriage's Domain." *Yale Journal on Regulation* 35 (special issue): 991–1026.

Chapter 5

Beyer, S. 2015. "How Miami Fought Gentrification and Won (for Now)." *Governing: The Future of States and Localities,* July 2015. www.governing.com/columns/urban-notebook/gov-miami-gentrification.html.

Clegg, N. 2020. "Combating COVID-19 across Our Apps." Facebook, March 25, 2020. https://about.fb.com/news/2020/03/combating-covid-19-misinformation.

Conger, K., and N. Scheiber. 2020. "Kickstarter Employees Vote to Unionize in a Big Step for Tech." *New York Times,* February 18, 2020. www.nytimes .com/2020/02/18/technology/kickstarter-union.html.

Correal, A. 2010. "El Barrio Tenants Win against Landlord." Movement for Justice in El Barrio, April 12, 2010. http://movementvsdawnayday.org/en /articles/el-barrio-tenants-win-against-landlord.

Costanza-Chock, S. 2020. *Design Justice: Community-Led Practices to Build the Worlds We Need.* Cambridge, MA: MIT Press.

Fields, D. 2015. "Contesting the Financialization of Urban Space: Community Organizations and the Struggle to Preserve Affordable Rental Housing in New York City." *Journal of Urban Affairs* 37 (2): 144–65.

Gajanan, M. 2018. "Mark Zuckerberg's Net Worth Skyrocketed as He Testified to Congress. Here's How Much He Earned." *CNN,* April 11, 2018. http://money.com/money/5235718/mark-zuckerberg-net-worth-Face-book-cambridge-analytica-congress-testimony.

Garcia, I. 2016. "A Puerto Rican Business District as a Community Strategy for Resisting Gentrification in Chicago." *Plerus* 25, 79–99. https://revistas .upr.edu/index.php/plerus/article/view/5196.

Gould-Wartofsky, M. 2008. "El Barrio Fights Back against Globalized Gentrification." *CounterPunch,* April 22, 2008. www.counterpunch.org /2008/04/22/el-barrio-fights-back-against-globalized-gentrification.

Haughney, C. 2009. "Tenants Struggle as a British Landlord Goes Bust." *New York Times,* December 21, 2009. www.nytimes.com/2009/12/22/nyregion /22dawnay.html.

Hays, M. 2016. "The One-in-Six Rule: Can Montreal Fight Gentrification by Banning Restaurants?" *Guardian,* November 16, 2016. www.theguardian .com/cities/2016/nov/16/one-in-six-rule-can-montreal-canada-fight-gentrification-banning-restaurants.

Heart of the City. 2013. "Google Bus Block." December 9, 2013. www .heart-of-the-city.org/google-bus-block---dec-9.html ——dec-9 .html.

Kang, C., and K. P. Vogel. 2019. "Tech Giants Amass a Lobbying Army for an Epic Washington Battle." *New York Times,* June 5, 2019. www.nytimes .com/2019/06/05/us/politics/amazon-apple-facebook-google-lobbying .html.

Koerner, B. 2018. "It Started as an Online Gaming Prank. Then It Turned Deadly." *Wired,* October 23, 2018. www.wired.com/story/swatting-deadly-online-gaming-prank.

Lewis, T., S. P. Gangadharan, M. Saba, and T. Petty. 2018. *Digital Defense Playbook: Community Power Tools for Reclaiming Data.* Detroit: Our Data Bodies.

Lingel, J. 2012. "Occupy Wall Street and the Myth of Technological Death of the Library." *First Monday* 17 (8). https://doi.org/10.5210/fm.v17i8.3845.

Lotman, M. 2018. "The Disclaimer." *Technoskeptic* 1 (1): 1–5.

Madrigal, A. 2019. "The End of Cyberspace." *Atlantic,* May 1, 2019. www.theatlantic.com/technology/archive/2019/05/the-end-of-cyberspace/588340.

Riga, A. 2016. "Bylaw Limiting Restaurants Now Applies to All of Notre-Dame St." *Montreal Gazette,* November 18, 2016. https://montrealgazette.com/news/local-news/bylaw-limiting-restaurants-now-applies-to-all-of-notre-dame-st.

San Francisco Municipal Transportation Agency. 2019. "Commuter Shuttle Program." www.sfmta.com/projects/commuter-shuttle-program.

Smiley, L. 2019. "The Porch Pirate of Portero Hill Can't Believe It Came to This." *Atlantic,* November 1, 2019. www.theatlantic.com/technology/archive/2019/11/stealing-amazon-packages-age-nextdoor/598156.

Solnit, R. 2013. "Diary: Google Invades." *London Review of Books* 35 (3). www.lrb.co.uk/v35/n03/rebecca-solnit/diary.

Woodcock, J. 2019. *Marx at the Arcade: Consoles, Controllers, and Class Struggle.* Chicago: Haymarket Books.

Index

Abbate, Janet, 76
advertising, 37–38, 40, 83, 104
Africa, Janine, 111
age discrimination, 56–57
AI Now, 116
Airbnb, 57, 69
algorithms, 17, 33–34, 38, 58, 104–5
allyship, 98
Amazon: corporate headquarters,
    46–47; lobbying by, 109; market
    domination of, 2; success
    narrative of, 68; user-name
    policies, 37; workforce diversity
    and, 61
Ames, Morgan, 45
Ankerson, Megan Sapnar, 46, 76
anonymity, 35
anti-gentrification activism. *See*
    resistance; urban anti-gentrification
    activism
antitrust law, 64–65, 121
Apple, 2, 109
Arment, Marco, 29
Associated Bank, 8
attention economy, 40

Aupperlee, Aaron, 58
Automattic Inc., 30

backbone networks, 79–80, 91
Baker, Jonathan, 65
Baker, Kevin, 14
BBSs (Bulletin Board Systems), 27,
    80, 121
Berman, David, 76, 85
Beyer, Scott, 101–2
Bezos, Jeff, 68
Big Tech: belief systems of, 43, 44–45,
    50–51, 56–57, 63; corporate head-
    quarters, 2, 43; corporate strategies,
    62; countercultural roots of, 51–52;
    definition of, 121; gentrification
    characteristics and, 15–17; internet
    role of, 19; post-recession boom,
    48–49; private transit systems, 49,
    100–101; products of, 57; resistance
    involvement, 52–54, 98; resistance
    within, 44, 106; resources of, 12;
    shareholder accountability, 14,
    68–69; Silicon Valley as exemplar
    of, 44–45; and urban gentrification,

Big Tech *(continued)*
2, 43–44, 46–52, 62, 100–101. *See also* Big Tech workforce; business models
Big Tech workforce: homogeneity of, 2–3, 43–44, 55–61; support staff, 53, 54; unionization, 3, 106
Bing, 2
Black Girls Code, 116
Blakeley, Phil, 99
Blendoor, 57–58
BME (Body Modification E-Zine), 23, 25–29, 32, 34
Bowker, Geoffrey, 74
boyd, danah, 35
Brock, Andre, 39
Bronx Coalition for a Community Vision, 113
Bruns, Axel, 13
Brunton, Finn, 41
Buckmaster, Jim, 67
Burning Man, 51
Bush, George W., 85–86
business models, 61–70; alternative, 66–67; antiregulation, 3, 45, 69, 86; and countercultural groups, 32; and cyberlibertarianism, 62; and Great Recession, 62–63; IPO model, 68–69; ISPs, 80–84; and monopolies, 44, 63–66; and profit motives, 1, 14, 43, 66–69, 105–6; and resistance, 69–70, 97, 105–6; success narratives, 68–69, 70, 105–6

Cable Act (1984), 92
California ideology, 121. *See also* cyberlibertarianism

Cambridge Analytica, 18, 96, 108–9
capitalism: and Big Tech belief systems, 45, 51; and gentrification as metaphor, 16; monopolies and, 64; and profit motives, 66–67; and resistance, 94, 111; and urban anti-gentrification activism, 69
Carceral Tech Resistance Network, 116
Center for Digital Democracy, 83
Chavez, Yolanda, 54
climate change, 101n
Color of Change, 113
Comcast, 83
commercialization: and advertising, 37–38, 40, 83, 104; and counter-cultural groups, 32; and data brokers, 38–39; and infrastructure, 72; ISPs and, 76, 80–84, 90; as key feature of digital gentrification, 15; and mesh networks, 90; and urban gentrification, 13–14. *See also* business models
Community Justice Land Trust, 93
community land trusts, 93
Commuter Shuttle Program, 101
Consentful Tech Project, 116
Correal, Annie, 99
countercultural groups: and Big Tech roots, 51–52; and digital displace-ment, 27–29, 30–31, 32; and early internet, 24–27; and user-name policies, 35–37, 110
COVID-19 pandemic, 9, 53, 105
Cox Communications, 83
Craigslist, 67–68
crime, and mesh networks, 88

Curtis, Sophie, 66
cyberlibertarianism, 45–46, 62, 121

dark fiber networks, 91–95
Data & Society, 116
data brokers, 39, 40, 41, 82, 83
Davis, Andrew, 46
Dawnay Day Group, 99
de Blasio, Bill, 89
Defense Advanced Research
    Projects Agency, 78
Demand Progress, 116
Department of Housing and Urban
    Development (HUD), 8
Detroit Community Technology
    Project, 117
digital culture: and digital redlining,
    41–42; and displacement, 3, 30–33;
    early internet, 26–27; and
    gentrification as metaphor, 17;
    and online communities, 36–37
Digital Defense Playbook (Lewis,
    Peña Gangadharan, Saba, and
    Petty), 39
digital displacement: and counter-
    cultural groups, 27–29, 30–31, 32;
    and digital culture, 3, 30–33; and
    digital platform domination, 3, 22;
    and ISPs, 73, 80–81, 84; as key
    feature of digital gentrification, 15;
    and online communities, 11–12;
    platform user base, 30–32, 33
digital infrastructure: dark fiber
    networks, 91–95; definition of, 74;
    internet role of, 19; mesh
    networks vs. ISPs, 86–90, 95;
    physical components of, 19, 71–72,
    79–80, 84, 87; social nature of,

74–75. *See also* internet service
    providers
digital platforms: advertising
    dependence, 37–38, 40, 104;
    algorithms used by, 17, 33–34, 38,
    58, 104–5; broad reach of, 27; and
    countercultural groups, 28, 30–31;
    and data brokers, 39, 40; definition
    of, 124; and digital displacement,
    11–12; discrimination by, 22, 23,
    38–42, 57–58, 104, 107; and
    displacement, 30; early failures,
    24; and filter bubbles, 13; history of,
    23–24; internet role of, 19; and
    isolation, 33–35; lobbying by, 109;
    market domination and, 2, 22,
    63–64, 66; misinformation on, 105;
    and online communities, 12, 26,
    28–29; politics of, 110–11; resistance
    within, 44, 55; size of, 17, 23; and
    success narratives, 68; user data
    controls, 28, 30–31, 105; user-name
    policies, 35–37, 38, 56–57, 110;
    workforce homogeneity, 55–57, 59,
    61. *See also* digital displacement;
    digital platforms; *specific platforms*
digital privacy: and ISPs, 81, 82; and
    resistance, 39, 83, 97, 98, 106, 108,
    109
digital redlining, 38–42
D'Ignazio, Catherine, 57
disability access, 94–95
discrimination: and algorithms, 23;
    commercialized, 22; and data
    brokers, 83; digital redlining,
    38–42; in hiring, 56–57; in housing
    markets, 8, 38–40; resistance to,
    57–58, 104, 107

displacement. *See* digital displacement; physical displacement

doxing, 106

drag communities, 35–36

Driscoll, Kevin, 76

Dropbox, 51

Dunbar-Hester, Christina, 92–93

Duolingo, 58, 59

early internet: and countercultural groups, 24–27; and innovation, 23–24, 63; and ISPs, 73, 76; military influence, 15, 76–77; optimism about, 10–11, 34, 37, 63, 87; oversight, 73, 76, 77–78

economic inequality. *See* inequality

18 Million Rising, 116

Electronic Frontier Foundation, 117

eminent domain, 8

Empower, DC, 113

Eubanks, Virginia, 39

Facebook: broad reach of, 27; Cambridge Analytica and, 18, 96, 108–9; content algorithms, 33–34, 104–5; and countercultural groups, 28; and digital redlining, 39–40; lobbying by, 109; market domination of, 2, 63, 66; misinformation on, 105; and online communities, 12, 26, 28–29; resistance within, 55; size of, 17, 23; success narrative of, 68; user data controls, 28, 105; user-name policies, 35–37, 110; workforce homogeneity, 55, 56, 59

Fair Housing Act, 40

FCC (Federal Communication Commission), 85–86, 92, 93, 122

fiduciary responsibility, 68, 122

Fifth Avenue Committee, 114

Fight for the Future, 117

filter bubbles, 33–35; definition of, 13, 122; resistance to, 105; and tech products, 57; and workforce homogeneity, 57, 61

Finley, Klint, 85

flipping houses, 8, 122

Florida, Richard, 47

4chan, 12

Free Press, 117

Garcia, Ivis, 102

gentrification. *See* urban gentrification

Glazer, Amihai, 47

Google: lobbying by, 109; market domination of, 2, 63–64; resistance within, 44; solution attempts by, 52; user-name policies, 37; workforce homogeneity, 55–57, 61

Gould-Wartofsky, Michael, 99

Grace Hopper Conference (2017), 59

Great Recession (2008), 8, 44, 48, 62–63, 99, 103

Greenstein, Shane, 77, 79, 80

Guardian, 51–52, 56

Haleguoa, Germaine, 91

Hays, Matthew, 102

Heart of the City, 100–101, 103

Hern, Alex, 56

Ho, Vivian, 52

homelessness, 50–51, 89

housing markets: and Big Tech corporate headquarters, 49; Big Tech solution attempts, 52–53; discrimination in, 8, 38–40; and

investment properties, 6–7; and resistance, 9, 52, 53, 99–100
Hu, Tung-Hui, 72
Humboldt Park Redevelopment Area (HPRA), 102–3
Hurricane Sandy, 89

inequality: and isolation, 34; and ISPs, 83–84; and online safety, 106–7; and physical displacement, 4–5, 7, 49; and urban gentrification, 3. *See also* discrimination
initial public offering (IPO) model, 68–69, 122
Innclusive, 57
Instagram: broad reach of, 27; and digital displacement, 30; and monopolies, 63; and online communities, 12; size of, 23
internet: access to, 73, 81, 83–84, 85–86; attitudes toward, 17–18; democratic potential of, 87; policies for, 75–76; user perceptions of, 66; vs. web, 75–76. *See also* early internet; Internet Service Providers
Internet Relay Chat (IRC), 27, 122–23
internet service providers (ISPs): business models, 80–84; commercialization of, 76, 80–84, 90; dark fiber networks, 91–95; definition of, 123; and digital displacement, 73, 80–81, 84; and digital privacy, 81, 82; history of, 73, 78–81; mesh networks and, 86–90, 95; and monopolies, 76, 80–82, 83–84; and net neutrality, 84–86; and physical displacement, 90; power of, 72–73

investment properties, 6–7, 123
IPO (initial public offering) model, 68–69, 122
IRC (Internet Relay Chat), 27, 122–23
IRL social networks, 12–13, 26, 34, 38, 123
isolation: and filter bubbles, 13, 33–35, 57, 61, 105, 122; and IRL social networks, 12–13, 34; as key feature of digital gentrification, 15; and urban gentrification, 12, 22; and workforce homogeneity, 57, 61
ISPs. *See* internet service providers

Johnson, Steven, 43

Kalanick, Travis, 68
Karp, David, 29
Keller, Justin, 50
Khan, Lina, 64–65
Klein, Lauren, 57
Kulwin, Noah, 63

LA Tenants Union, 11, 108, 114
Lane, Ben, 8
Larratt, Rachel, 28–29
Larratt, Shannon, 26–27
last mile problem, 84, 90, 123
Lewis, Tamika, 39, 83, 97
Lindeman, Tracey, 6
lobbying, 109
local laws and policies: and Big Tech corporate headquarters, 46, 47; and gentrification as metaphor, 18–19; and resistance, 53–54, 101–2, 103, 109–10; and urban gentrification, 4, 8, 10, 14, 66, 72, 109

Lotman, Mo, 74, 96
Luckie, Mark, 55, 59

Macrina, Alison, 69
Madrigal, Alexis, 97
MediaJustice, 117
meritocracy, 45, 51, 61, 123
mesh networks, 86–90, 123
Meyersohn, Nathaniel, 62
Microsoft, 2, 44, 61, 63–64
MJB (Movement for Justice in El
   Barrio), 99–100, 103
monopolies: and Big Tech business
   models, 44, 63–66; digital
   platform market domination, 2,
   22, 63–64, 66; and ISPs, 76, 80–82,
   83–84. *See also* antitrust law;
   digital displacement
MOVE, 111
Movement for Justice in El Barrio
   (MJB), 99–100, 103
Musk, Elon, 68

names. *See* user-name policies
National Coalition for Asian Pacific
   American Community Develop-
   ment, 114
National Community Reinvestment
   Coalition, 114
National Hispanic Media Coalition,
   117
National Low Income Housing
   Coalition, 114
National Science Foundation (NSF),
   73, 78, 80
net neutrality, 84–86, 104, 109, 124
Newmark, Craig, 67
Next City, 114

NIMBY attitudes, 50
Nissenbaum, Helen, 41
Noble, Safiya, 39
Nuestra Comunidad Development
   Corporation, 114
NYC Mesh, 117

Obama, Barack, 82, 85–86
Obfuscation (Brunton and Nissen-
   baum), 41
One Laptop Per Child project, 45
online harassment, 106–7, 109
Open Technology Fund, 117
Open Technology Institute, 118
Our Data Bodies, 39, 83, 97, 107, 118

Pao, Ellen, 63
Pariser, Eli, 13
Paseo Boricua, 102, 103
Peña Gangadharan, Seeta, 39, 83, 97
People's Open, 89, 118
Perez, Gina, 4
Petrusich, Amanda, 37
Petty, Tawana, 39, 83, 97
Philadelphia Tenants Union, 115
physical displacement, 3–4; and
   countercultural groups, 51–52; and
   inequality, 4–5, 7, 49; and
   investment properties, 6–7; and
   ISPs, 90; as key feature of urban
   gentrification, 10, 15, 22; process
   of, 11
Pichai, Sundar, 54
Pickard, Victor, 76, 85
platforms. *See* digital platforms
Policy Link, 49
profile names. *See* user-name
   policies

profit focus. *See* commercialization
proprietary networks, 66
ProPublica, 40
Public Knowledge, 118
public radio, 92
public television, 92

racism, 5, 8, 55, 56, 83. *See also*
    discrimination; inequality
Radical Reference, 118
recession (2008), 8, 44, 48, 62–63,
    99, 103
Red Hook WiFi, 88–89, 90, 118
Reddit, 12, 63
redlining, 8, 38–42, 124
regulation: antitrust law, 64–65, 121;
    business models opposed to, 3, 45,
    69, 86; net neutrality laws, 84–86,
    104, 109; and resistance, 103,
    108–10; and urban anti-gentrifica-
    tion activism, 53
Renninger, Bryce, 30
Resilient Just Technologies, 118
resistance, 96–111; and allyship, 98;
    anti-internet gentrification
    resources, 116–19; and antitrust
    law, 64–65; and bias, 57–58; Big
    Tech involvement, 52–54, 98; and
    business models, 69–70, 97,
    105–6; coalition-building, 36,
    94–95, 102, 110; community radio,
    92–93; and content diversity,
    104–5; corporate pressure,
    100–101, 103; and dark fiber
    networks, 91–92, 93–94; and
    digital privacy, 39, 83, 97, 98, 106,
    108, 109; and digital redlining, 41;
    direct action campaigns, 94–95,
103; and disability access, 94–95;
    and housing markets, 9, 52, 53,
    99–100; infrastructure reclama-
    tion, 91–95; legal action, 99–100,
    103; and local laws and policies,
    53, 101–2, 103, 109–10; and mesh
    networks, 86, 87, 88–89, 90; and
    net neutrality, 84–86, 104, 109;
    and online safety, 106–8, 109; and
    platform discrimination, 104, 107;
    and platform politics, 110–11; and
    regulation, 103, 108–10; and
    success narratives, 105–6; and tax
    abatement, 53–54; technology, 15,
    54; unionization, 3, 106; within Big
    Tech, 44, 106; and workforce
    homogeneity, 58–59. *See also*
    urban anti-gentrification activism
Right to the City Alliance, 115
Romano, Aja, 31
Rosenthal, Tracy Jeanne, 11

Saba, Mariella, 39, 83, 97
segregation, 12, 34. *See also* isolation
sexism, 56, 58–59
ShowTech, 60
Silicon Valley, 44–45, 48–51, 52–54.
    See also Big Tech
Silicon Valley Rising, 115
Skycoin, 82
Smiley, Lauren, 107
Smith, Neil, 51
Snowden, Edward, 18
social media platforms. *See* digital
    platforms
Solnit, Rebecca, 100
Solon, Olivia, 51–52, 63
South Bronx Unite, 115

Square, 53
Star, Susan Leigh, 74
Starosielski, Nicole, 72
Statista, 64
STEM fields, 60-61
Stop LAPD Spying Coalition, 118
success narratives, 68-69, 70, 105-6
surveillance, 18, 81, 82, 87, 97, 107-8
Surveillance Technology Oversight
    Project, 119
swatting, 106
Szmigiera, M., 64

tax abatement, 8, 10, 109; and Big
    Tech corporate headquarters, 47,
    48; definition of, 124; and digital
    platforms, 46-47; and personal
    choices, 20; and positive views of
    gentrification, 6; and resistance,
    53-54
tech industry. *See* Big Tech
Tech Learning Collective, 119
techno-determinism, 45, 124
Techno Skeptic, 96
techno-skepticism, 96-97, 124
tenant committees, 99-100, 103
Tesla, 61, 68
TikTok, 30
Time Warner Cable, 83
Tor Project, 119
TransTech, 119
Tribal Digital Village, 119
trolling, 106
Trump, Donald, 86
Tufekci, Zeynep, 40
Tumblr, 23, 29-33, 34, 106
Turner, Fred, 46, 51
Twitter, 26, 53

Uber, 68, 69
unionization, 3, 106
urban anti-gentrification activism,
    10, 99-103; and Big Tech
    corporate headquarters, 46; Big
    Tech involvement, 52-54; and
    capitalism, 69; community land
    trusts, 93; and gentrification as
    metaphor, 20-21, 98; and
    infrastructure, 100-101; and local
    laws and policies, 101-2, 103, 109;
    and mesh networks, 89-90; and
    regulation, 53; resources, 113-15;
    and tenant committees, 99-100,
    103
Urban Displacement Project, 115
urban gentrification: and Big Tech, 2,
    43-44, 46-52, 62, 100-101; and
    commercialization, 13-14; contrib-
    uting forces, 4, 7-9; definitions
    and key features, 4, 9-10, 22, 122;
    and digital redlining, 39-40;
    increase in, 6; and inequality, 3;
    and investment property, 6-7; and
    local laws and policies, 4, 8, 10, 14,
    66, 72, 109; as metaphor, 1-3,
    10-11, 15-17, 18-19, 46, 65-66; and
    monopolies, 65-66; positive views
    of, 3, 6, 47, 51; and power, 4-5, 9,
    103; and privilege, 49-50; and
    safety, 107-8; and segregation, 12;
    as spatial concept, 5, 16; and tax
    abatement, 6, 8, 10, 47, 48, 109.
    See also physical displacement
Urban Reform Institute, 115
U.S. Congress, 108
U.S. Department of Defense, 78
U.S. Department of Education, 60

U.S. Department of Housing and Urban Development (HUD), 39–40
U.S. Equal Employment Opportunity Commission, 56
U.S. Government Accountability Office, 34
user-name policies, 35–37, 38, 56–57, 110

values. *See* digital culture
Verizon, 83
Vine, 30
von Ahn, Luis, 58

Wall Street, 8–9
Walmart, 84
Warren, Elizabeth, 65
web, 75–76. *See also* internet
Weiner, Anna, 57–58

WhatsApp, 63
Wheaton, Wil, 31
Wired, 43
Women's Community Revitalization Project, 93, 115
WordPress, 26, 30
Worker Solidarity Network, 111
workforce. *See* Big Tech workforce
World, 78
World Wide Web (WWW), 75–76. *See also* internet
Wu, Tim, 65, 85

Yahoo!, 30
YouTube, 13, 23, 104, 105

Zapier, 52–53
zoning laws, 102, 109
Zuckerberg, Mark, 68, 108–9
Zukin, Sharon, 4

Founded in 1893,
UNIVERSITY OF CALIFORNIA PRESS
publishes bold, progressive books and journals
on topics in the arts, humanities, social sciences,
and natural sciences—with a focus on social
justice issues—that inspire thought and action
among readers worldwide.

The UC PRESS FOUNDATION
raises funds to uphold the press's vital role
as an independent, nonprofit publisher, and
receives philanthropic support from a wide
range of individuals and institutions—and from
committed readers like you. To learn more, visit
ucpress.edu/supportus.